LIFE IN PICTURES

ELVIS

LIFE IN PICTURES

ELVIS

Marie Clayton

Bath New York Singapore Hong Kong Cologne Delhi Melbourne

First published by Parragon in 2010

Parragon
Queen Street House
4 Queen Street
Bath, BA1 1HE, UK

Copyright © Parragon Books Ltd 2010
For photographs copyrights see pages 254–255

Produced by Atlantic Publishing

A catalogue record for this book is available from the British Library.
ISBN 978-1-4454-0540-7

Printed in China

Contents

Introduction

Elvis Presley burst onto the American music scene in 1956, although he had been well known locally around Memphis for some time beforehand. He quickly became synonymous with the new rock 'n' roll music and teenagers everywhere took him to their hearts. His sensual performing style whipped his female fans into a frenzy, which initially caused much criticism in the press – but the resulting publicity did his career no harm at all. After he was drafted and did his service in the US army, without complaint or favors, opinion about him in the press began to change, and on his return his new, mature style helped him to reach an even wider audience.

Not content with being perhaps the world's most popular singer, he also moved into acting and soon took Hollywood by storm. During his career he made 31 movies – all of which were a success at the box office – and in the middle of the 1960s he was the highest-paid actor in Hollywood. After he returned to the concert stage in the 1970s his shows in Las Vegas were legendary, and he was soon dubbed the "World's Greatest Entertainer."

Life in Pictures: Elvis charts the fascinating life of Elvis, right from his humble beginnings to his tragic death as a superstar and its aftermath. The exciting collection of photographs featured not only show him performing, but also include candid shots documenting his private life and a comprehensive selection of stills taken during the making of his films. Many of the photographs are not clearly dated in the archives, but in this book they have been carefully placed in context with what was happening in his career at around the time they were taken. The pictures are accompanied by detailed and perceptive captions, which give a rounded portrait of the world's most famous singer. Elvis Presley was a phenomenon and his legacy continues to captivate people even today – the King may be dead, but his memory lingers on.

CHAPTER ONE

Love Me Tender

When Elvis Presley was born on January 8, 1935, few people could have predicted that he would go on to live the "American dream." His family were so poor they could not afford proper medical care; as a result his older twin brother, Jesse, was stillborn—a loss that was never to be forgotten, either by his mother, Gladys, or by Elvis himself. In the following years the family moved around Mississippi. Vernon, Elvis's father, had a series of jobs and Gladys too often had to work to support the family; and, when things got too tough, they simply moved on. Elvis was very close to his mother—particularly after his father was imprisoned for several months for forging a check—and she was very protective of her only surviving child.

Elvis grew up in a series of homes close to black neighborhoods and, as a result, enjoyed black R&B, jazz, and soul music from his earliest years, never regarding it as something separate from his own life as most white people did at the time. His family was closely involved with the church—particularly Gladys, who often attended several times a day—and Elvis was brought up to the sounds of gospel music, joining in as soon as he was able. Gladys also listened to country and western music on the radio at home, and Elvis was quick to learn all the songs.

Despite their circumstances, Gladys insisted that Elvis learn good manners and show respect to his elders—a grounding that stayed with him for the rest of his

life. She constantly impressed upon him that he was special and different from other people. He grew up rather shy and dreamy, something of a loner, and music became a release from the constraints of his life. His family had no money to pay for lessons so he taught himself to play the piano and learned guitar from family friends. With a good memory for words and music, he was able to sing or play a song after hearing it just once or twice. He entered his first singing competition at the age of 10, coming second and winning $5 plus free admission to some fairground rides.

Moving to Memphis in 1948, the Presleys lived near Beale Street, the legendary home of the blues. Moving his body while he was singing was something Elvis had already learned from gospel singers but, in Memphis, he also learned from the way the black singers he saw there moved. He came to admire their sense of style and color, and in his teens began to develop his own look, which combined bold colors and sharp tailoring with long, slicked-back hair and sideburns. Typical outfits included a bolero jacket bought from Lanskys—a tailor on Beale Street—and pants with a bright stripe down the side of the leg, and a bright-pink suit teamed with white suede shoes. It was very different from the cropped, preppy look

Opposite: A publicity picture taken around the time of *Love Me Tender*.

of most other teenagers of the time. At first, Elvis aspired to be a gospel singer, but he also played hillbilly music and soon developed his own sound—a sound that was unlike that of any of the well-known singers of the time, but that later became known as rockabilly and then rock 'n' roll.

Sam Phillips and Marion Keisker had opened a recording studio in Memphis, mainly to record the music played by black artists. Sometime during the summer of 1953, Elvis—by that time working as a truck driver—turned up on their doorstep to record something and to let Sam hear him sing. Nothing happened for some time, but eventually Sam called him back and teamed him with two more experienced musicians: guitarist Scotty Moore and bass player Bill Black. After much rehearsing and several false starts as they found their way together, the three of them recorded an old blues number by Arthur "Big Boy" Crudup: "That's All Right, Mama." A few days later, Dewey Phillips—one of the most popular and influential disk jockeys in the area—played the record around 14 times in just one evening (the exact number is uncertain) and told his listeners it was sure to be a hit. The results stunned everybody: thousands of phone calls requested more of the new singer and, much to Sam Phillips' surprise, Elvis's music was not only popular with the white audience, but with the black one too.

At first, Scotty Moore managed the group but, later, DJ Bob Neal took over, making bookings for live appearances at clubs and concerts, and later organizing local concert tours. They began to play regularly at the Eagle's Nest in Memphis, but Sam Phillips also managed to get a booking at that mecca of country singing, Nashville's Grand Ole Opry. It was unheard of for an unknown singer to play the Opry, and all of them were thrilled; unfortunately, though, the audience was not ready for their new style and Elvis was advised to stick to driving trucks. He never played there again. The *Louisiana Hayride*, broadcast on KWKH from Shreveport's Municipal Auditorium, proved more welcoming. Elvis and the Blue Moon Boys were an instant hit and were quickly invited back. They began to tour almost full-time—often driving all night, playing a concert then driving on to the next

show, with just a few snatched hours of sleep in the back of the car. Despite this, Elvis always seemed constantly active and rarely tired; when he finally did sleep, though, it would be for 11 or 12 hours.

Now he was releasing records, and playing regularly at the *Louisiana Hayride* and other well-known venues, Elvis began to feel he was really on his way. He already had a large group of fans, who would arrive whenever he was due to appear. He was still a local phenomenon, however, and he needed another push to achieve national popularity. That push was not long coming—in late 1954, Elvis met Colonel Tom Parker for the first time, and he soon had plans for the still rather naive young singer who was driving audiences wild.

The Colonel had started out in carnival, but moved into showbusiness when he became the manager of singer Eddy Arnold. When he met Elvis, he was working as a promoter and his astute business practices, promotional skills, and attention to detail were already famous. Although his title was an honorary one, conferred by a state governor, he insisted on using it at all times. Having arranged a few tours for Elvis, and noting the audience reaction, he began to take over, maneuvering everyone else out of the way.

With the Colonel's help, Elvis transferred to the national stage and was soon headlining shows across the country. Women went wild as he shook his hips or jiggled his legs—movements a world away from those of other singers of the time, who hardly moved at all while they sang. Some religious leaders took exception to his "lewd" actions onstage, and called for both Elvis and his music to be banned. At a concert in Jacksonville, Florida, in May 1955, fans rioted, leaping onto the stage and attempting to tear off Elvis's clothes; this soon became a fairly regular occurrence. Elvis loved all the attention and often encouraged his fans—both onstage and off. Despite his polite, shy, and humble image, Elvis had a reputation for never turning a woman away from his door. He dated several different women regularly—even when his steady girlfriend, Dixie Locke, was still waiting for him at home. She eventually split up with him, although not because of the time he spent with his other women; she was dismayed that the demands of touring left him with no time to spend with her.

Gladys had always wanted her son Elvis to be someone special, but now that he was she found it hard to cope with his fame. He was always away touring instead of at home with her, and she was distressed by the overheated reaction of his female fans. Elvis had been her main emotional support for many years; now he was no longer around and her problems began to escalate.

By November 1955 Colonel Parker had arranged for RCA to buy Elvis's contract from Sam Phillips, who needed funds to develop his other singers—including Johnny Cash, Roy Orbison, Carl Perkins, and Jerry Lee Lewis. The following year RCA released its first Elvis single, "Heartbreak Hotel." To the disappointment of RCA executives, it was a very different sound to anything Elvis had recorded before and they began to wonder if they had made a costly mistake. However, it was a massive hit, going to No. 1 in the charts and, by mid-1956, Elvis was bringing in over half of RCA's total income.

Elvis also made several appearances on *Stage Show* on CBS TV, reaching an audience across the entire country for the first time. The Colonel soon became Elvis's sole and exclusive manager. He had recognized the fact that Elvis appealed to a new audience, as the repressed youth of America found their own identity and began to rebel against authority. Naturally, these teenagers wanted their own music, preferably something their elders did not approve of, and rock 'n' roll fitted the bill perfectly. With this audience came a vast new market just waiting to be tapped. Part of Elvis's appeal was that he was a mass of contradictions: he appeared shy and polite but, onstage, moved in a way that drove women crazy; he belted out rock 'n' roll numbers but sang gospel with true feeling; he was quietly spoken and loved his mother, but was also an audacious youth who encouraged teenagers to rebel.

Elvis himself could never understand why there was a problem. He moved the way he did because that was what seemed natural to him; gospel was his own first love, but rock 'n' roll was what the audience wanted; and

he never saw himself as a rebel because he had simply grown up with the kind of music he sang. Record sales boomed on the back of all the publicity. The Colonel already had his eye on the next move and, in April 1956, Elvis did a screen test and soon had a movie contract with Paramount Pictures.

Despite everything else that was going on, Elvis was still touring almost nonstop—including a two-week run at the New Frontier Hotel in Las Vegas. Unfortunately, this was not a success as the venue's middle class audience was more used to sophisticated entertainers like Frank Sinatra and didn't take to the raw energy of Elvis's rock 'n' roll. However, it was in Vegas that Elvis met Liberace, who was to become a close friend, and who advised him on how to dress to please his audience. Elvis's style soon began to change, and he not only sorted out his skin problems but also had his teeth capped.

In August 1956, Elvis began work on his first movie, *Love Me Tender*, a drama set just after the Civil War. Elvis played the youngest son of a farming family, who marries the girlfriend of his eldest brother after everyone assumes that the brother is dead. The Colonel was astute enough to retain the publishing rights to the film's score, rather than handing them over to the studio and, after Elvis appeared on *The Ed Sullivan Show*, advance orders of two million were received for the single "Love Me Tender." The film opened in 500 theaters across the US that November, and was a huge hit despite an unenthusiastic response from the movie critics.

The Colonel was also quick to realize the potential for Elvis-related merchandise, and set up companies to sell a Presley product range that included jeans, charm bracelets, stick-on sideburns, hair pomade, bubblegum cards, and even lipstick. At the center of all this fuss, however, Elvis was becoming increasingly isolated, his movements restricted, and was already beginning to lay down the roots of the lifestyle that would eventually lead to his destruction.

Getting started

Above: Elvis appeared at the *Louisiana Hayride* for the first time in October 1954. The performance went down well and he and the Blue Moon Boys were given a contract to appear every Saturday night. The *Hayride* was broadcast live from the Municipal Auditorium in Shreveport, and reached 28 states: it was much more innovative than the Opry and became a haven for new talent.

Opposite: An early publicity picture. Elvis's first single, "That's All Right, Mama," was released in July 1954 and quickly sold 20,000 copies. His second Sun single, "Good Rockin' Tonight," issued in September 1954, was as great a success as the first. Elvis, Scotty Moore, and Bill Black soon had regular concert bookings and Sam Phillips arranged for them to appear at Nashville's Grand Ole Opry. Unfortunately the audience was more used to traditional country singers, and the response was lukewarm. Afterwards, the show's talent coordinator, Jim Denny, suggested Elvis should go back to driving a truck.

One night in Tampa

Above and opposite: Elvis performs with his brand new Martin D-28 acoustic guitar and bass player Bill Black (above) at Fort Homer Hesterly Armory, Tampa, Florida, on July 31, 1955.

Elvis soon developed a huge following that mainly consisted of teenage girls, and by mid 1955 his devoted army of fans would attend wherever he was performing. Elvis loved the attention and was quick to encourage the girls in the audience, teasing and swiveling his hips until they became so hysterical they would try to grab him before he left the stage. Their jealous boyfriends could be even more dangerous.

Right: The young Elvis pictured on a train.

First chart success

Above: Belting out a song in the recording studio. The release of "Baby, Let's Play House" caused a major stir because of its suggestive lyrics, but the fans loved it and it quickly went into the national charts—the first Elvis record to do so. Soon afterward, Elvis signed a management contract with Colonel Tom Parker.

Opposite: An early portrait in which Elvis looks very natural—after Elvis met Liberace in Las Vegas, he made many changes to the way he looked. Liberace had told him that he should dress to please the audience, and Elvis took his advice to heart.

Back at Sun Studios

Left: Robert Johnson, Sam Phillips, and Leo Soroka pictured with Elvis at Sun Studios.

Below: Elvis poses with Colonel Tom Parker. Elvis came to the attention of Tom Parker, a showbusiness promoter, in October 1954. Parker quickly realized that audiences' reactions to Elvis were something special.

Opposite: Elvis photographed in his dressing room during rehearsals for *The Milton Berle Show.*

Singing with the Jordanaires

Above: Elvis rehearses with gospel quartet the Jordanaires, Burbank, California, June 4, 1956. Elvis had been introduced to the backing group in 1955, before he became a star, and had been impressed by their work. When he began to record with RCA, he asked that the Jordanaires back him.

Opposite: Elvis with fans on the set of *The Milton Berle Show*.

Speculating about romance

Above: Judy Powell Spreckels, former wife of sugar heir Adolph Spreckels, manages to catch Elvis after *The Milton Berle Show*. The two of them exchanged rings, and the press speculated that they were enjoying a romance.

Opposite: Irish McCalla, the star of *Sheena, Queen of the Jungle*, holds Elvis hostage. They appeared together on *The Milton Berle Show* in spring 1956.

Heartbreak Hotel

Opposite: A publicity picture of Elvis. After he signed with RCA at the end of 1955, Elvis began to move away from rockabilly into true rock 'n' roll. It was the start of a gradual progression in his style and in his music, always moving on to try to reach a wider audience. Released in 1956, "Heartbreak Hotel" was the first Elvis record that became a hit for RCA. Elvis had first heard the song in 1955 at a disk jockey convention and had immediately decided he wanted to record it. Songwriters Mae Axton and Tommy Durden had written the song after reading a newspaper article about a young man who had committed suicide, leaving a note that said, "I walk a lonely street." The song became the first of his records to sell a million copies and his first No. 1 hit.

Hound Dog

This page and following pages: The *Milton Berle Show* that featured Elvis's first appearance was broadcast from the deck of the USS *Hancock*, which was docked at the San Diego Naval Station. Despite the novelty of the location, it was his second appearance on the show, in June of that year, that brought more publicity. During his second appearance on *The Milton Berle Show*, Elvis sang "Hound Dog" for the first time on television. It was a new song, but the audience loved it and Elvis responded to their enthusiasm by taking his hip-swiveling performance to greater heights. "Hound Dog" was released in July 1956 and sold over five million copies by the end of the year. As he reached the final part of "Hound Dog," Elvis slowed down the tempo of the song and proceeded to thrust his hips in time to the music in a distinctly suggestive way. The studio audience were driven to a frenzy of excitement, screaming and laughing at the same time. That evening, for the first time in the season, *The Milton Berle Show* topped *Sergeant Bilko* in the ratings.

Critics' response

Right and below: The day after *The Milton Berle Show* was broadcast, many critics condemned Elvis's performance. John Crosby of the *New York Herald Tribune* said he was "unspeakably untalented and vulgar." Jack O'Brian of the *New York Journal-American* wrote of "... a display of primitive physical movement difficult to describe in terms suitable to a family newspaper ..." and Ben Gross said in the *Daily News* that '... he gave an exhibition that was suggestive and vulgar, tinged with the kind of animalism that should be confined to dives and bordellos."

The Steve Allen Show

Opposite: Soon afterwards Elvis appeared on *The Steve Allen Show*, but Allen insisted his performance be toned down and that he should wear a tuxedo. The fans were furious, and picketed the NBC studios the following morning.

Following pages: Elvis first appeared in Las Vegas in April 1956, but the engagement was not a great success. However, he met Liberace there for the first time and they went on to become lifelong friends.

A new, confident Elvis

Opposite: On stage at Russwood Park, in July 1956. When Elvis first appeared, dressed all in black except for red socks and tie, the fans rushed out of their seats and swept forwards toward the stage. The last few months had given Elvis a new confidence, so he was able to tease and control the crowd without letting anything get out of hand.

Above: The Colonel always had a supply of photographs for the fans to buy—and Elvis was happy to sign them. In later years, he rarely went out in public because he was constantly mobbed by his fans.

Hollywood, here I come

In August 1956, filming began on Elvis's first movie, *Love Me Tender*, which was being made by Twentieth-Century Fox. After his screen test for Hal Wallis, Elvis had been offered a three-picture deal by Paramount—but they had no suitable vehicle for him, so had loaned him to Twentieth Century Fox. Elvis had an excellent memory, and he not only knew his own part before he arrived in Hollywood, but had also learned the entire script by heart. His costars were Richard Egan and Debra Paget (above), both experienced actors, and Elvis was very nervous but also extremely willing to learn. The producer, David Weisbart, had produced *Rebel Without a Cause* and Elvis was excited to meet him as he had deeply admired James Dean.

Down on the farm...

Opposite: A publicity picture for *Love Me Tender*. Originally entitled *The Reno Brothers*, *Love Me Tender* was a drama set just after the Civil War. Elvis played the youngest son of a farming family, who marries the girlfriend of his eldest brother after everyone assumes that the brother is dead. When the older brother returns, the family is torn apart and Elvis's character is killed. Since the producers worried that the fans would be upset if their idol died, an alternative ending was shot, in which he survives. In the end they stayed with the original storyline, but Elvis appears again at the end, singing the title song over the credits.

Natural acting ability

Above: Elvis pictured on set with costar Debra Paget. Producer David Weisbart told reporters that Elvis had the same smoldering appeal for teenagers, and the same impulsive nature, as James Dean. He advised Elvis not to have acting lessons but to rely on his greatest asset—his natural ability.

Left: Although *Love Me Tender* had only four musical numbers, they were carefully worked into the storyline.

Charming the birds from the trees ...

Debra Paget played the elder brother's girlfriend in *Love Me Tender*. Elvis had a big crush on her, but she did not return his regard—although she thought he was "very sweet." Elvis was well-liked by his costars, and they went out of their way to help him in the new and strange world of movie-making. Richard Egan, who played the elder brother, said of him later, "That boy could charm the birds from the trees."

The theme song, "Love Me Tender," was based on a Civil War ballad called "Aura Lee." Elvis was better known for more raunchy numbers, but he sang the ballad with real feeling. When it was released in September 1956 as a single the song was a great hit, so the name of the film was quickly changed to *Love Me Tender* before it was released. This was the only movie in which Elvis appeared where the part was not specifically written for him—in fact Robert Wagner was originally under consideration to play the role.

Time revealed that RCA had record-breaking advance orders of one million for the single, and even before the movie opened the record reached No. 1 in the *Billboard* Top 100.

A quiet charm

Opposite: After he began to become well known nationally, almost every aspect of Elvis was publicly criticized—his dress, the raunchy way he moved, his ducktail hair, his sideburns. Because of all this negative publicity he soon developed an image as a dangerous rebel, who would encourage young people to defy their elders—but teenagers loved him partly because their elders did disapprove. Elvis himself could never understand the fuss; he did not try to cause offense and almost everyone who met him was soon won over by his quiet, shy charm. The Colonel could see the power of the new teenage market and for a while was content to exploit it—he created all kinds of gimmicks to keep the fans happy and the free publicity also boosted record sales.

Above: Elvis on the set of *Love Me Tender*. Director Robert Webb was very patient with his fledgling star, taking him aside between shots to go over the scenes and breaking the lines down to show the emphasis.

Back home in Tupelo

Opposite: Nick Adams, an actor and Hollywood hustler who had become Elvis's friend, introduced him to Natalie Wood. The papers reported that Elvis and Natalie were having a sizzling romance, but they usually went around in a gang with Nick and his other friends. Natalie described Elvis as "a real pixie … he has a wonderful little-boy quality."

Above: In September, Elvis appeared at a homecoming concert in Tupelo. Before the concert began a parade was held in his honor, but the Colonel vetoed the suggestion that Elvis should ride in it because of concerns over security. Main Street was decked with a giant banner that said, "Tupelo Welcomes Elvis Presley Home." Elvis's parents, Vernon and Gladys, were there to see his triumph—though Gladys later told a friend that it had made her uncomfortable to remember how poor they had been when they lived there.

A new romance

Opposite: Elvis and June Juanico, whom he had first met in her hometown of Biloxi when he had played the Keesler Air Force Base in 1955. Almost a year later they met again in Memphis and dated for several months through the summer of 1956.

Right: Rehearsing for *The Ed Sullivan Show*. By this time Elvis appeared relaxed and confident.

Appearing on Ed Sullivan

Left: Ed Sullivan discusses a few points with Elvis during preparations for his second appearance on *The Ed Sullivan Show* in October 1956. Although Sullivan had declared that Elvis would never appear on his show, he later backed down and signed him for three performances. Elvis was paid a total of $50,000 for his appearances—which was considerably more than the sum the Colonel had originally asked for when he first approached Sullivan and had been turned down. When the first show was broadcast in early September, actor Charles Laughton acted as host since Sullivan was recovering from a car accident.

Fooling with Bill Black

Opposite and right: Despite all the controversy, Elvis enjoyed appearing before an audience, along with Scotty Moore, DJ Fontana on drums, and Bill Black on bass. At the end of Elvis's third appearance on his show, Ed Sullivan told the audience that he thought Elvis was "a real decent fine boy." While Elvis played to the girls, Bill Black often played the fool with his bass in the background. Sometimes he pretended to dance with it, at others he rode it like a horse—which always elicited a laugh from the audience. The ratings for the Sullivan show—and every other show—invariably went up when Elvis appeared.

Star guest

Left: Liberace talking to Elvis in the audience on the opening night of his concert at the Hotel Riviera in Las Vegas. Elvis was taking a few days off in Vegas, staying at the New Frontier Hotel.

Just pure gold

After the concert, Liberace and Elvis swapped jackets and instruments and fooled around for the cameras. Liberace's jacket was a gold cutaway, and was the inspiration for the famous $2,500 gold-lamé suit that the Colonel had made up for Elvis by Nudie Cohen the following year. Liberace told journalists, "Elvis and I may be characters—but we can afford to be." Elvis always sent flowers for Liberace's opening nights.

November 1956

Opposite: When *Love Me Tender* was released in November 1956, a huge cutout of Elvis as Clint Reno was unveiled on a New York City theater. Thousands of fans turned out to see the movie—despite the fact that the critics' reviews of Elvis's performance were derisive and condescending. The reviews were hardly surprising, given the bad publicity Elvis had been getting throughout the year, but they were very unfair. For an inexperienced actor, Elvis acquitted himself very well.

Right: By the end of 1956 the poor boy from Tupelo was poised to become an international star of both stage and screen.

CHAPTER TWO

Treat Me Nice

By the beginning of 1957, Elvis was accompanied by armed security guards wherever he went, since he could no longer so much as step into the street without being mobbed by fans, causing a riot. He was constantly surrounded by members of his entourage, a close-knit circle of men who were both companions and support group. They fueled his ego, rushed to fulfill every whim, and were on hand 24 hours a day to sing gospel or to party. Often badly behaved, they appeared arrogant to outsiders, and they soon became known in most circles as the "Memphis Mafia."

After Elvis had played a concert, he and the Mafia would usually party all night with local musicians—and plenty of girls too. To relax, he sang gospel music or played the piano. He could now afford to buy whatever he wanted to eat—but had a weakness for junk food, particularly cheeseburgers, sliced banana and peanut butter sandwiches, greasy doughnuts, crisply burned bacon, fried or mashed potatoes and dark-brown gravy. A diet of this kind of food was beginning to cause weight problems—although he was still burning off a great many calories in nervous energy. He also often walked in his sleep when he was anxious or upset, which gave those around him cause for concern about his safety. During the unhappy booking at the New Frontier Hotel in Las Vegas in 1956, his companion Red West regularly sat up all night in case Elvis walked straight out of the open window.

Despite Elvis's burgeoning health problems, the hours spent on the road, the constant lack of sleep, and his poor diet, he always seemed to find plenty of energy when it was time to take the stage.

For some time, rumors had been spreading that Elvis was about to be drafted. Early in 1957 he reported to the Kennedy Veterans Hospital in Memphis for his pre-induction US Army physical; he was classed 1-A and therefore eligible for military service, although the authorities said it was unlikely he would be called within the next six months. The Army also confirmed that the famous hair—Elvis's pride and joy—would have to come off. Meanwhile, there was another film to be made, *Loving You*, about a singer in search of fame. It also starred Lizbeth Scott and Wendell Corey—established actors who would not feel the need to eclipse the new kid on the block. Gladys and Vernon came to visit their son on-set and were filmed for one scene, watching the concert that takes place at the climax of the story.

One of the first major purchases Elvis had made with his new-found wealth was a home for his parents,

Opposite: Dr. Fred Jeff Burford, of St. Petersburg, Florida, gives Elvis his pre-induction physical. Dr. Burford gave the final approval that made Elvis eligible for the draft.

in Audubon Drive, Memphis. Unfortunately, fans often turned up in their hundreds to hang around outside, and the neighbors soon tired of this constant intrusion. Elvis decided he needed a property with some seclusion, so Vernon and Gladys set out to find one. As soon as they saw Graceland they fell in love with it, and quickly called Elvis to come and see it for himself. A Georgian colonial-style mansion, Graceland had been built in 1939 for Dr. Thomas Moore and his wife, and named after Mrs Moore's great-aunt Grace, who had owned the land. It was set in acres of ground, and placed well back from Highway 51—later to be renamed Elvis Presley Boulevard. Elvis was immediately enthusiastic about the property, and the purchase was completed within a week. Renovations were soon underway, as well as essential structural repairs. Elvis had a swimming pool added, and installed a real soda fountain and specially made gates with a musical note motif. He had the interior entirely redecorated, mostly in dark colors with glitzy touches. Over the years, further additions included a recording studio, a large trophy room, stables, fenced-in fields, and vegetable patches.

His mother was really happy at the idea of moving in and wanted her own chicken house and hog pen, but things did not turn out quite the way she expected. She soon missed the company and the casual get-togethers that had been a major part of her life in town, and began to feel increasingly isolated. Elvis was constantly touring or filming, and Vernon seemed to be busy much of the time. Even when Elvis was there he was constantly surrounded by other people, as Graceland had also become home to various members of the Memphis Mafia, along with a changing population of band members, back-up singers, and starlets. This meant that Gladys had little time alone with her son.

Although Elvis continued to perform regularly, it was becoming somewhat hazardous to attend his concerts because of the wild behavior of some of the fans—and even he couldn't hear himself sing over the noise they made. There was also growing discontent in his backing group, as Bill Black, Scotty Moore, and drummer

DJ Fontana were still only being paid a flat rate of $200 a week when they were working, with a retainer of $100 a week when they were not. Since they were by no means working full-time but, at the same time, were banned from appearing other than with Elvis, their incomes were severely limited. DJ had come in later than the others and had always been a salaried employee so he was relatively content, but the Blue Moon Boys had been with Elvis from the beginning and felt they deserved better. Apart from the money problem, they were bored in Hollywood, where they had little to do, and found they were increasingly being excluded from direct contact with Elvis himself.

Shooting was soon to begin on another movie, *Jailhouse Rock*, in which Elvis played a bad boy who reformed in prison and went on to become a famous singing star. It was one of his best films, with specially commissioned songs by Leiber and Stoller, who came out to Hollywood to oversee the recording. Unfortunately, one of the Colonel's stipulations in his management of Elvis had been to make sure that the writers of his songs had to hand over a percentage of their royalties; word of this soon got around, seriously limiting the selection of songs Elvis was offered in later years—to the point that it began to damage his career.

During rehearsals for the opening dance sequence in *Jailhouse Rock*, a porcelain cap came off one of Elvis's teeth and he managed to inhale it. The cap lodged in one of his lungs and he was taken to hospital where doctors managed to retrieve it by inserting an instrument via his vocal cords and down into the lung itself. Elvis was hoarse for a few days afterwards but, to everyone's relief, his voice soon recovered.

Elvis got on very well with Judy Tyler, his costar in *Jailhouse Rock*, but, as she was newly married, she wasn't interested in any sort of romantic attachment with him. Tragically, she and her husband were killed in a car accident soon after filming finished, and Elvis was so upset he could never watch the finished picture. Another important relationship also hit the rocks in this period. The DJ Dewey Phillips, who had first played "That's All Right, Mama" and been so instrumental in launching Elvis's career, came out to visit him in Hollywood. Elvis played him a single that was about to be released, "Teddy Bear," from his previous film, *Loving You*. Phillips loved it and, against Elvis's explicit instructions, took a copy of the record and played it on air on his return to Memphis. Because the record had not even been released, Phillips' scoop infuriated both the Colonel and record executives, and Elvis and Phillips had a major falling-out. Although they were later to patch things up, their friendship was never quite the same.

Back in Memphis, Elvis began dating Anita Wood, a blonde former beauty queen whom he had first seen on the television show *Top Ten Dance Party*, broadcast on WHBQ. Although he continued to see other women throughout their relationship, the romance was fairly serious; she was a regular visitor to Graceland and got on very well with Elvis's mother. He gave Anita a sapphire and diamond ring, which she publicly told reporters was merely a friendship ring—although she and many others believed privately that it was meant as much more.

At the same time, Gladys herself was not only depressed but was becoming increasingly unwell—she had a liver problem and suffered badly from fluid retention, so her ankles and legs often swelled. It was not like her to complain about her problems, but according to several members of the Memphis Mafia it was around this period that she began to drink heavily and in secret.

By September 1957, Scotty Moore and Bill Black decided they had accepted poor salaries and bad treatment for long enough. There seemed no sign of any imminent change, so they both resigned. They had played a large part in Elvis's success, but felt that he had not shared it with them—while he had become wealthy, they were in debt. Elvis made a belated offer of more money, but it was too little too late as, in the meantime, the newspapers had seized on the story and run an interview with both musicians. Elvis felt betrayed, and immediately began auditioning to find new backing players. Although he found two good musicians, it just wasn't the same and, after a time, both sides swallowed their pride and Scotty and Bill came back—but only for an improved daily rate of pay.

Elvis was scheduled to begin work on his fourth movie, *King Creole*, at the end of December, but in the middle of that month he finally received his draft notice. Previously, representatives from the military authorities had offered him special status: the Navy planned to form a company round him that would entertain the troops; the Air Force suggested he could spend his time touring recruiting centers. Elvis turned down their offers, saying that he just wanted to be treated like any other soldier—he was aware that any sign that he was being treated differently would be reported in the press and cause a great deal of resentment. Publicly he announced that he was happy to go and do his duty, to give back a little in return for what America had done for him. Privately, though, he was very worried, and told friends that he feared a long absence might cause fans to forget him and end his career. He did not have to leave immediately, however; on behalf of Paramount he requested a 60-day deferment to allow him to film *King Creole*, pointing out that, unless he did so, the studio would lose the large sum of money it had already spent on pre-production. The request was granted, and filming began.

By now, Elvis was earning a fortune—although no one will ever know exactly how much. Even Elvis himself had no idea how much the Colonel received for any of his performances or films; he wasn't interested in the business details. As long as the promises the Colonel made to him were kept, in a professional capacity he was content to be where he was supposed to be and do what he was told to do. As well as the management contract with Elvis, the recording deals, the music publishing, and the film contracts—all of which many people say gave the Colonel more than his fair share—some people suggest that he also took millions of dollars on the side. He always had promotional items on sale outside concerts and the hotels where Elvis was staying, and was quick to come up with new gimmicks if he thought the fans would buy them. Now "his boy" was going into the Army and would not be available for two years. The Colonel was nothing if not resourceful, however, and would soon come up with a way to turn the situation to his advantage.

Loving You

The storyline of Elvis's second film, *Loving You,* was loosely based on his own life. Elvis played Deke Rivers, an unknown but talented singer with a new sound. Lizabeth Scott played a hard-headed music promoter who exploits him for his appeal to teenage audiences but the press soon label him as a bad influence and a rebel. After Deke manages to convince people that he is really a fine, upstanding young man, the movie ends happily. Dolores Hart (opposite) played the romantic interest.

Friends and family

Left: Elvis with Las Vegas dancer Dorothy Hammond.

Below: Gladys and Vernon are pictured with just a few of the hundreds of gifts from fans that Elvis received on his 22nd birthday. The fans often gathered outside his parents' home in Memphis and the neighbors were beginning to get annoyed with the constant intrusions.

Opposite: Elvis in *Loving You*. Originally to be called *Lonesome Cowboy,* the title of the movie was changed shortly before production began to allow the inclusion of the Leiber and Stoller song "Loving You."

Happy days

Right: Elvis and Dolores Hart share a joke while making *Loving You*, which was filmed in the early part of 1957. Elvis had his hair dyed black for the part, and it looked so good he continued to dye it for the rest of his life. Its natural color was more a dark blond.

Below: Elvis with actress Judy Tyler and musician Bill Black, on bass, during the making of *Jailhouse Rock*.

Jailhouse Rock

Opposite: *Jailhouse Rock* was a low-budget movie shot in black and white, with stylized sets, but the simple settings enhanced the serious storyline. Many believe it was one of the best movies Elvis ever made—and it made a great deal of money for MGM and for Elvis himself, who received a large percentage of the profits. Elvis threw himself into the dance routine with such abandon that he swallowed one of the temporary caps from his teeth. It lodged in his lung and had to be recovered with surgery. For a while there was some concern that Elvis's voice would be affected, but the fears proved to be groundless.

Bad boy image

Right: In his third movie, *Jailhouse Rock*, Elvis plays Vince Everett, who is sent to prison for killing a man in self-defense. His character is hot-blooded and bitter over the unfair sentence, and becomes an angry, sullen, and brooding young man. The fans are therefore treated to several scenes of a very passionate and provocative Elvis. *Jailhouse Rock* played on Elvis's bad boy image. While Vince Everett is in jail, he learns to sing and play the guitar from another inmate. Afterwards Vince becomes a famous rock star, but is not a particularly pleasant person until an accident stops him in his tracks. He becomes a nice guy who falls in love with the heroine, Peggy van Alden, played by Judy Tyler.

Opposite: Elvis and Anne Neyland, a former Miss Texas who also appeared in *Jailhouse Rock*, exchange a smoldering look. They dated during the shooting of the movie and for a few weeks afterward.

Proud owner of Graceland

Left: The new owner of Graceland stands proudly next to one of the columns of the entrance portico. The renovations and decorations that Elvis wanted were to cost almost as much again as the house itself—and one of his priorities was to create "the most beautiful bedroom in Memphis" for his mother.

Devastated by Judy's death

Above and opposite: Elvis with Judy Tyler, who played Peggy van Alden, in *Jailhouse Rock*. Peggy is the record promoter who helps Vince to stardom and falls in love with him—but haughtily refuses to respond to his advances until he becomes a reformed man. Elvis and Judy were great friends during the shooting of the movie—but Judy was newly married and not interested in romance. A few weeks after shooting finished, she and her husband were killed in a car accident. Elvis was devastated and did not attend the movie's premiere.

Following pages: Elvis in a scene from *Jailhouse Rock*, which many believe was one of the best movies Elvis ever made.

A professional touch…

Elvis performs in the dancing scenes in *Jailhouse Rock*. During the filming of the movie Elvis became friendly with professional dancer Russ Tamblyn, who gave him a few tips to sharpen up his dancing style. For the big dance sequence performed to the title song, Elvis was backed by a team of professional dancers. He had initially been wary about the whole idea, but choreographer Alex Romero watched Elvis move around naturally when he was singing, and then worked the steps up into a routine. Elvis was much more comfortable and enthusiastic with the final result, and it looks very like the way he normally moved on stage. The single "Jailhouse Rock"/"Treat Me Nice" was also a great success and sold over three million copies in 12 months in the US. It was the first Elvis record to reach No. 1 in the charts in Britain.

Parting is such sweet sorrow …

Above: Anita Wood hugs Elvis good-bye as he prepares to leave on a whirlwind tour of the Pacific northwest. Anita was a former beauty queen, who was now appearing on *Top Ten Dance Party* on WHBQ. She had just won the Mid-South Hollywood Star Hunt and was also about to leave, for the finalists' competition in New Orleans. The two of them were together for several years—although that didn't stop Elvis from dating a number of other women during the same period.

Right: Elvis pictured at the time of the tour, which covered five cities in four days, so there was little time for rest and relaxation. Elvis and Tom Diskin, his road manager, were accompanied by George Klein, Lamar Fike, and Cliff Gleaves. By this stage, Elvis had a string of hits including "All Shook Up," "Teddy Bear," and "Jailhouse Rock" which were all released during 1957.

Opposite: A publicity photograph. During the tour there were riots in nearly every city, and in Spokane, Washington, fans broke onto the infield of the Memorial Stadium and tried to steal the soil because Elvis's feet had touched it. In Vancouver, a contingent of Canadian Mounties had been drafted in to hold back the crowd of 25,000, but they were quickly overwhelmed.

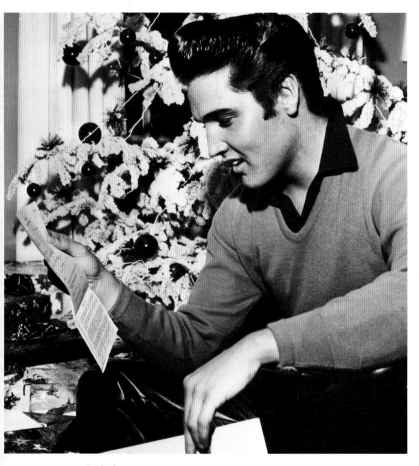

Drafted!

Above: Just before Christmas 1957, Elvis received his draft notification and although he collected the notice himself to avoid publicity, the press soon got wind of it. He told reporters that he was happy the situation was finally resolved and that he was happy to return something to the country that had given him so much. When photographers wanted to picture him with the notice a minor panic ensued, as Elvis couldn't remember where he had put it.

Opposite: Actress Venetia Stevenson was the daughter of Anna Lee and director Robert Stevenson. She and Elvis dated on and off through 1957 and 1958, but their relationship was never serious.

Screaming and swooning

Left: When *Jailhouse Rock* was released, the fans were ecstatic. The response of the movie theater audiences matched that of the fans who attended concerts, each making so much noise that no one could hear Elvis sing. The movie went on to make a profit within only three weeks.

Above: Elvis got himself into trouble when he was accused of pulling a gun on Private First Class Hershel, after the young Marine claimed Elvis had insulted his wife. Since Elvis had never met Mrs. Hershel—and the gun was a prop, which he had brought back from Hollywood—the whole affair was settled out of court.

Opposite: By 1958 Elvis had become one of Hollywood's most bankable stars.

CHAPTER THREE

It's Now or Never

Early in January 1958, Elvis flew to California to record the soundtrack for *King Creole* and then begin filming. The film told the story of a young man who dropped out of college and became involved with gangsters, but then overcame adversity to become a famous singer. It had some similarities with Elvis's life and was one of the few of his own films that he liked. Both the director, Michael Curtiz, and Elvis's co-star, Walter Matthau (who played the heavy), were impressed with how Elvis approached the role, and believed he would go on to become a great actor. Elvis himself was determined to do his best, as it might be his last film. Who knew what would happen when he returned from the Army?

Two weeks after shooting had finished, Elvis was finally inducted into the US Army. He arrived early at the draft board, accompanied by Anita Wood, and various friends and relatives, to be greeted by the Colonel and a group of journalists and photographers from the press. After a short media interview, Elvis was taken off to the Kennedy Veterans Hospital with his fellow recruits to be checked out, but even his medical examination was conducted in the glare of publicity. The bus taking Elvis on to Fort Chaffee, Arkansas, was followed by hundreds of cars and, at a scheduled stop for coffee and sandwiches, there were so many people already waiting that no one was able to leave the bus.

The commander in charge at Fort Chaffee had agreed that the press would have full access, so Elvis made his bed for the cameras, had breakfast with the Colonel and newsmen, and was photographed having his hair cut, and being issued with and wearing his uniform. He was assigned to the Second Armored Division at Fort Hood in Texas for basic training, where he was also to receive advanced tank instruction. Having seen the circus around Fort Chaffee, those in charge at Fort Hood decided to take a different approach. The media were given one day of free access, after which the new recruit was strictly off-limits. It was the first time Elvis had been on his own, away from his family and friends. Although he was homesick, he kept his feelings to himself and buckled down to learning how to be a soldier. After some initial difficulties, the other soldiers eventually accepted him as one of the boys.

The Colonel discovered that a soldier could live off base after basic training if he had dependants in the area. So Vernon and Gladys quickly packed up and moved to Killeen, the nearest town to the base. At first they lived in a trailer, but since Vernon's mother, Minnie Presley, and one of the Memphis Mafia, Lamar Fike, had come with them, they soon found a house

Opposite: Elvis shows off his Army haircut.

to rent instead. Elvis drove back and forth to the base each day, and at weekends Anita often came to stay.

Everything seemed to be progressing smoothly, but Gladys was feeling increasingly ill and the hot Texas summer wasn't helping. In August she decided to return to Memphis to see her doctor, who rushed her off to hospital. Despite many tests it was unclear exactly what the problem was, but it was certainly serious and Elvis was called. He was initially unable to get leave, but after threatening to go AWOL was given a pass on compassionate grounds. Although she appeared to rally when Elvis appeared, Gladys died of a heart attack two days later.

Elvis was inconsolable, and not embarrassed to show it. He and his father wept openly, and Elvis told the press that his mother's death had broken his heart. They had been so close, despite the time they had spent apart over the last few years while he had been building his career; she had been the one person he could always trust to be there for him. Her body was laid out at Graceland so that friends and relatives could pay their last respects. Elvis couldn't stop touching her, patting her hands, kissing her, and pleading with her to come back. Those close to him eventually talked him away and he was given a sedative to help him sleep. At the funeral, Elvis almost collapsed and old friends rallied round to help him get through the next few days, but just over a week after his mother's death he had to return to Fort Hood and the Army.

There were several more weeks of training to get through, and Elvis was a diligent recruit and managed well despite his grief. The following month, his unit was transferred by train to New York, where it was to join the ship that would take it to Germany. Elvis's embarkation was marked by the usual media circus—at a press conference he answered questions about the Army, marriage, his mother, and his music, and was photographed going up the gangplank with a borrowed duffel bag. Elvis was not going abroad alone, though—he had arranged for Vernon, his grandmother, and Memphis Mafia members Lamar Fike and Red West

to come over separately and set up home near his base. The Colonel was to stay behind in America to make sure "his boy" was not forgotten while he was away.

Although he had never been abroad before—let alone toured there—Elvis was greeted by thousands of ecstatic fans when his ship docked at Bremerhaven. His unit transferred by train to Friedberg, where he was to spend his service, and, after a press conference in the canteen, all media were banned from the US base. A day later, Elvis's entourage arrived in the country and, after renting rooms in a couple of hotels for several months, settled in a rented house at Goethestrasse 14, which became Elvis's home when he was not on duty for the rest of the time he was in Germany.

Although Elvis did the usual soldiers' duties and went on maneuvers while in the Army, he had an easier life than many soldiers. Lamar and Red looked after his uniform for him, and he had enough money to buy spare kit so he always looked smart. During several of his leaves, he and his friends traveled to Paris, where they visited famous nightclubs such as the Folies Bergère, the Lido, and the Moulin Rouge, and the showgirls were always ready to party.

Elvis dated several German girls while he was in their country, but there were no serious relationships. He was still seeing Anita, and she came over to visit him several times. However, at a club in Wiesbaden in November 1959 he was introduced to Priscilla Beaulieu. The stepdaughter of an Army officer, Priscilla was only 14 but was very pretty and Elvis enjoyed her company. They saw each other regularly during the rest of the time he was there and he met her parents, but since he was also still seeing other women, their relationship was by no means exclusive. Vernon also met someone—Dee Stanley, the wife of a sergeant and mother of three young boys. She and Vernon soon began an affair, which Elvis was deeply upset about since it was only just over a year since his beloved mother had died.

Meanwhile the Colonel was keeping things going in America. Before he left, Elvis had recorded several songs, so there were still some records to release in his absence. The Colonel also made sure there was a steady stream of stories in the press about Elvis and his Army career—complete with a few pictures of him looking handsome in uniform. He sent out messages on Elvis's behalf and made sure the fans were kept satisfied; although he was careful not to flood the market so that they would still want more. He was so successful that more than one million advance orders for any record Elvis cared to make on his return had already been received, and several new film projects were agreed.

In March 1960, after two years, Elvis's Army career was finally drawing to a close. He had been promoted twice, and now held the rank of sergeant—although pictures taken on his return show his uniform with an extra stripe, denoting the rank of staff sergeant, which he did not earn. Before he left Germany, Priscilla came to bid him a tearful farewell and he promised to call her, but she was not certain she would ever see him again. Back in America, as he went through the motions of being discharged, the media circus began to gear up again, with coverage of him receiving his final pay check—and immediately handing it over to the Colonel—waving to crowds in his uniform, and the journey back home to Graceland.

Most people agree that his time in service changed Elvis—afterwards he was more mature and conservative professionally, and his music became more mainstream. However, there was also another and more serious change. According to several people who knew him at the time, Elvis had started to take amphetamines regularly. Apparently, he had first used them to help him stay awake during night maneuvers in Germany, but now took them on a daily basis—not only to keep him going but to help him stay slim. He had come out of the Army 15 pounds lighter than when he went in, but still tended to prefer junk food. Throughout his life, he disapproved of drug taking, but since the amphetamines were prescription drugs he did not regard them in the same light. The pills not only caused mood swings but also contributed to Elvis's growing disconnection from the normal world.

One of the first things the Colonel had lined up for his return was an appearance on a Frank Sinatra special, which was to be taped at the Fontainbleu Hotel in Miami Beach. Elvis caught a train down to Florida, and the track was lined with people for almost its entire length—his fans had not forgotten him. After the show, he went back into the studio to record new songs, and then to begin the soundtrack for a new movie, GI Blues. The film's storyline was lightweight and capitalized on Elvis's time in the Army. His character was a soldier who also happened to be a musician, and who fell in love with a cabaret singer. It was set in Germany, but all of Elvis's scenes were shot in Hollywood. It marked a change from his previous films in that he was no longer playing a bad boy who makes good, but a safe and wholesome character. He also completed another western, Flaming Star, in 1960 and began shooting Wild in the Country, both for Twentieth Century Fox; these movies allowed him to move away from his singing a little and tackle slightly more dramatic roles.

The Sinatra show was finally broadcast in May 1960, and the audience was split between those who loved Elvis's new, mature, laid-back style and those who wondered where the rebel rocker had gone. The doubters were heavily outnumbered, though. Elvis lost few fans and picked up many more, so he was still one of the most popular singers in America. At home, however, things were not so happy. Dee had divorced her former husband, and she and Vernon finally married, although Elvis refused to go to their wedding. The newlyweds moved into Graceland with Dee's three sons for a short time, but soon moved out again into a place of their own.

As he settled back into his old life, Elvis was still dating Anita but he was also seeing several other women on a casual basis. Despite her doubts, he did call Priscilla regularly, and they talked about her coming over to America to see him. It was not to happen for another two years.

Joining up

Left: Elvis celebrating his 23rd birthday, with a little help from two of his friends. His celebration that year was low key, as his imminent induction into the Army had put everyone in low spirits.

Below: Elvis kisses his sorrowful mother goodbye, watched by his father, just before he is inducted into the United States Army.

Leaving Memphis

Above: Many of Elvis's loyal female fans turn up to tell him they will not forget him while he is away, and Elvis happily chats to them and signs autographs. The press are constantly present, with the Army's permission—although when one photographer hides in the barracks at Fort Chaffee to try to get a picture of Elvis sleeping in his bunk, it is decided that things have gone too far and the hapless snapper is thrown out.

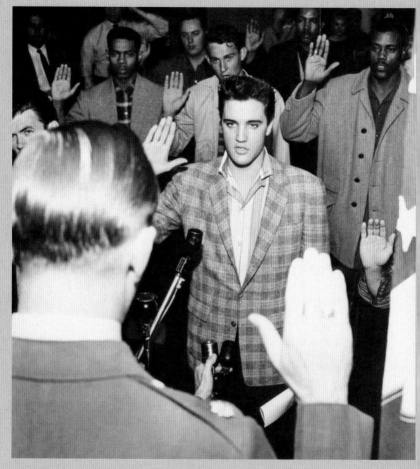

March 1958: You're in the Army now …

Above: Major Elbert P. Turner swears Elvis into the Army at the draft board in Memphis, Tennessee. The new recruit told reporters that he was dreading the haircut he would get the following day, but that he hoped he would be treated the same as everyone else.

Opposite: There were 55 reporters and photographers on hand to record the famous haircut. Elvis held up some of the hair for the press, and joked, "Hair today, gone tomorrow!" Later he was issued with $7 in partial pay; the reporters ask what he will do with all the money, and Elvis jokingly replies that he plans to start a loan company.

Shot three times

Above: The new-look Elvis faces the cameras. All the publicity surrounding the event got Elvis so flustered that he forgot to pay the barber his 65¢ fee, and had to be called back—much to his embarrassment.

Opposite: The Army shoots Elvis three times, when he gets his jabs for typhoid, tetanus, and Asian flu. As well as medical tests and a haircut, he also had to do five hours of aptitude tests and sit through a two-hour lecture on a private's rights and privileges.

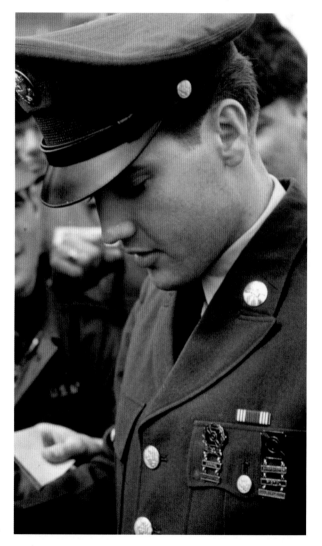

Kitted out for service

Opposite: Elvis tries on some snappy footwear and displays the latest design in Army fatigues. He dealt with all the press attention with great patience and good humor, only refusing to sign autographs while he was "in ranks."

It was soon announced that Elvis was to be assigned to the 2nd Armored Division at Fort Hood just outside Killeen in Texas, to do his basic training and advanced tank instruction. The 2nd Armored was General George Patton's famous "Hell on Wheels" outfit. Six of the other Memphis draftees were also to be sent to Fort Hood, where basic training would last for eight weeks. There was no sign of the press attention letting up, so the Army was beginning to rethink its policy of full access.

Right: Elvis signs some autographs.

In uniform

Above: Private Elvis Presley alights from the chartered Greyhound bus at Fort Hood in central Texas, after the day-long journey from Fort Chaffee in Arkansas. The bus had bypassed the usual stops in Dallas and Waxahachie, where hundreds of people had gathered. It finally stopped for lunch in Hillsboro, Texas, and two of the largest men were detailed to sit either side of Elvis. It was 25 minutes before anyone recognized him, but then a riot ensued as it took some time for everyone to get out of the building and back on the bus.

Left and opposite: As well as the Army fatigues, Elvis had been issued with a dress uniform. He later bought several spare sets of kit, which Memphis Mafia members Lamar Fike and Red West looked after for him when they were all in Germany. Elvis was always so well turned out that he won "Best-Dressed Soldier" several times.

Sneaking a preview

Left: During his leave, Elvis and his parents attended a sneak preview of *King Creole*, which was held in Memphis.

Below: Elvis was always happy to come down to the gates of Graceland to sign autographs and chat to the fans. When reporters asked him why he was wearing his uniform while on leave, he replied, "I'm kinda proud of it." He also told them that he had adjusted to Army hours and was now having trouble staying awake after midnight.

Previous pages: Vernon Presley admires his son's medals. Elvis had earned his marksman medal with a carbine and his sharpshooter medal with a pistol and was now Acting Assistant Squad Leader.

August 1958: Gladys is taken ill

Above: Elvis with his father. In August 1958, Gladys Presley was admitted to hospital. The diagnosis was uncertain, but her illness was serious enough for Elvis to be given compassionate leave. He went straight to the hospital, where Vernon was already staying—sleeping in a folding cot next to the hospital bed. His visit seemed to cheer Gladys up and for a time the doctors thought she might recover.

Gladys dies

Left: In the early hours of Thursday morning Gladys died of a heart attack. When reporters arrived at Graceland later in the day, they found Vernon and Elvis sitting on the steps of the house. Elvis, sobbing uncontrollably, told them that his mother was all they had lived for and that she had always been his "best girl."

Opposite above: Just over a week after the funeral Elvis had to return to Fort Hood to complete his basic training and a month later his unit left for Germany. Since 125 newsmen had arrived in New York to see him off, a press conference and photo opportunity were organized before he boarded the ship. His kit had already been loaded, so a borrowed duffel bag was quickly provided for the pictures.

Below: Although Elvis had never been in Europe, he already had fans there. At least 500 German teenagers arrived to welcome him when the ship docked at Bremerhaven. From the docks the soldiers caught a train to the base at Friedberg, near Frankfurt. Elvis waved to fans and to waiting newsmen as the train left the station.

Margit dates her "very nice boy"

Right: Elvis holding hands with Margit Buergin, a young typist with an electrical supply company in Frankfurt. She had waited outside his hotel to get his autograph and photographers had called for them to kiss. Elvis happily obliged, and he dated Margit several times afterwards. She was only 16, but looked older, and still lived with her mother. She told the press that she thought Elvis was "a very nice boy" and that she liked him very much.

Rocking with Bill Haley in Frankfurt

Above: Bill Haley was appearing in Frankfurt on October 23 and in Stuttgart six days later. Elvis went to see him both times, although he had to stay backstage during the show to avoid causing a riot. He told Haley that he was grateful for his help and encouragement in the early days—and that, without it, he might still be driving a truck.

Opposite: Elvis shaving at base camp in Grafenwöhr while on maneuvers. It was a cold, dismal, and muddy place near the border, but Elvis endured the same conditions as the other soldiers and turned out to be a resourceful and clever scout. He proved himself not only to his platoon sergeant but also to his fellow soldiers and was finally accepted by them as one of the boys. While he was away, Vernon met Dee Stanley and the two of them became close. Dee later divorced her Army husband and married Vernon, much to Elvis's disapproval.

On maneuvers

Left: Elvis and his fellow soldiers in the barracks at Friedberg. Elvis was assigned to Company C, a scout platoon, where he drove a jeep for Reconnaissance Platoon Sergeant Ira Jones. One reason that Company C was selected was because it spent much of its time on maneuvers, which would keep Private Presley well out of the public eye.

Opposite: Elvis demonstrates the equipment in his jeep to four-year-old Michael Jones, the son of his platoon sergeant, at an Open House held at the 3rd Armored Division headquarters in Friedberg in April 1959.

Below: The day after Elvis returned from maneuvers, he took possession of a secondhand white BMW 507 sports car that had previously been used by German racer Hans Stuck for demonstrations. He had also bought an old Cadillac for his father to use and a Volkswagen Beetle for the boys. The first Christmas in Germany was sad for everyone, not only because they were away from home but because it was the first without Gladys.

All teamwork but no touring

Opposite: During the time he was in Germany, Elvis never once appeared on stage or sang for a proper audience. He had been instructed not to do so by Colonel Tom Parker—partly so that he would not be treated differently, but also partly because the Colonel did not see why the Army should get for free what everyone else was prepared to pay a fortune for. Back home, the Colonel was using Elvis's absence and the shortage of material to up the ante in all his negotiations with RCA and the Hollywood studios.

Above: When a World War I memorial in a German village had to be moved to a new location, the US Army stepped in to help. Private Presley directed operations as the sections were lifted by crane. Later he told the press that he thought he and the other soldiers had worked pretty well as a team.

Promoted
to acting sergeant

Opposite: Elvis had already been promoted to the rank of Specialist Fourth Class, but in January 1960 he was promoted again to acting sergeant. He proudly shows off his new stripes to photographers.

Above and left: Elvis poses with an artillery gun. Russian leaders had dubbed him "Public Enemy Number One" and accused the US of using him as a weapon in psychological warfare.

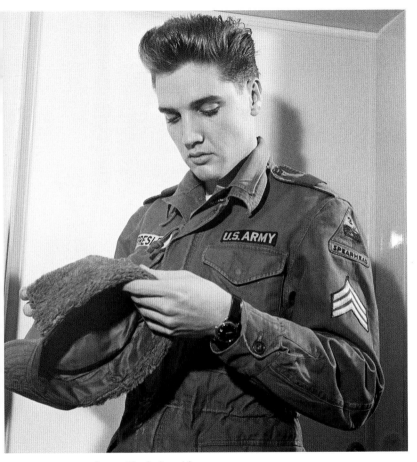

Sergeant Presley is no richer

Above: The advancement in rank carried no increase in pay, but since Elvis was considerably richer than most soldiers, this did not concern him!

Opposite: While he was in Germany, Elvis did not live on base with the other soldiers. His family and a couple of the Memphis Mafia were there with him and at first they stayed in a series of hotels. After a shaving cream fight and an incident when a small fire set off all the alarms, they were asked to move out, so Elvis rented a house. Here his grandmother was able to cook the kind of food he liked—and Elvis was often able to slip back home for lunch.

Back in the field ...

Above: Sergeant Elvis Presley warms his hands by the camp fire. By this time he had been made up to full rank and his platoon were back out on maneuvers at Grafenwöhr—and it was the middle of winter and bitterly cold. Elvis was looking forward to his discharge—he had only a couple months to go.

Left: Elvis and his fellow soldiers checking a map. He made several new friends in the Army, including Charlie Hodge who came to work for him in civilian life afterwards and stayed with him right to the end.

Elvis in Paris

Above: The Army was not all mud and guns—here Elvis enjoys a few days' R&R in Paris, where he stayed in the Prince de Galles hotel in Avenue Georges V with Lamar Fike, Charlie Hodge, and Rex Mansfield. They visited famous nightclubs such as the Moulin Rouge and the Folies Bergère and once took the entire chorus line of Bluebell Girls from the Lido back to their hotel. They had so much fun in Paris that Elvis decided to stay one more night, paying for a limousine to drive them all back to Friedberg the following day.

Right: Back in Germany Priscilla is pictured with an Elvis LP. All the newspapers referred to her as his 16-year-old girlfriend, but at the time she was still only 14—although she was very mature for her age. Her family had insisted on meeting Elvis before they would let her see him regularly, but were won over by his charm and sincerity.

Back to civilian life

Above: Donning his fatigues for the last time, Elvis studies himself in the mirror. He had survived
two years in the Army and was now about to go home again. He told most of his Army buddies that
he was looking forward to making more films and hoped to do more serious roles—but to closer
friends he confided that he was afraid the fans would have forgotten him.

The homecoming

Left: Elvis faces journalists at a last press conference in Germany in March 1960, before leaving for the US. He told newsmen that he had learned a lot from the Army and his commanding officer, General Richard J. Brown, gave him a special certificate for "cheerfulness and drive and continually outstanding leadership."

Below: The press were on hand again to record every step of the discharge proceedings. Here Elvis boards a bus at Fort Dix that will take him from his orientation lecture to the base finance building to collect his final pay.

Back to work—and play

Opposite and above: Lucky fan Barbara Ann Murray of Roselle Park, New Jersey, poses with Elvis.

With his hair already beginning to grow out of the regulation Army haircut, Elvis was beginning to look more like the King of rock 'n' roll again. He told reporters that he planned to rest at home—although in fact he had a busy schedule. He not only had a recording session planned, but also an appearance on The *Frank Sinatra Show,* and was soon to start shooting on a new film. Instead he told the newsmen about his newfound interest in karate, which he had been studying in Germany.

Right: Actress Tina Louise, who went on to become the star of *Gilligan's Island,* interviews Elvis for the cameras.

Official discharge

Above: Elvis was discharged from the Army in March 1960. Here he holds his certificate of discharge while signing a few autographs for his Army buddies.

Are You Lonesome Tonight?

Above: The Colonel reminds Elvis not to forget his commission—and Elvis hands him the entire $109.54.

Left: As well as appearing with Frank Sinatra, Elvis recorded some classic songs including "Are You Lonesome Tonight?" and "It's Now or Never" in the spring of 1960. "It's Now or Never" went on to sell nine million copies. The LP *Elvis is Back* was also released and stayed in the *Billboard* chart for 56 weeks. The fans soon resumed their old habits, and Elvis was almost besieged wherever he went.

Opposite: On his train journey down to Miami to record the Sinatra show, almost the entire route was lined with fans and press. Of course the Colonel had taken the trouble to let everyone know Elvis was coming, but it was still an amazing turnout for a singer who had not appeared in concert or recorded any fresh material for nearly two years.

GI Blues

Opposite and following pages: In May 1960, Elvis began filming *GI Blues*, a musical comedy in which he played a singer serving in the Army. The story borrowed heavily from recent events in Elvis's own life—his character is not only stationed in Germany, he is also in a tank division. The film was aimed at a general market rather than teenagers, and Elvis appears more mature and responsible. While filming was in progress, a stream of important visitors came to see Elvis on set. In just one day he welcomed the King and Queen of Thailand, the wife and daughter of the Brazilian President, and three Scandinavian princesses (opposite)—not to mention Pat Boone, Minnie Pearl, and Ernie Ford. The Colonel made sure that everyone knew that he was responsible for the royals—he was tirelessly dedicated to promoting anything that involved "his boy."

Above: Elvis with Bobby Darin, who was appearing at the Hotel Saharah at Las Vegas. Elvis was in Las Vegas on a short vacation, after filming on *GI Blues* was finished. During the weekend, he lost $10,000 at the craps tables.

Costarring Juliet Prowse

Opposite: Juliet Prowse watches Elvis try the double bass. Juliet Prowse was the girlfriend of Frank Sinatra—who was not amused when rumors of an affair with Elvis reached him. As well as Juliet, the film also starred Sigrid Maier, Leticia Roman, Robert Ivers, and James Douglas. It was the last movie in the original three-picture contract with Hal Wallis, but the Colonel soon began to negotiate another, similar deal.

Above: In his next film, *Flaming Star*, Elvis plays Pacer Burton, the son of a white settler and a Kiowa Indian woman, played by Dolores Del Rio.

Right: Elvis with Barbara Eden, who played his romantic interest in *Flaming Star*. She later went on to star in the television series *I Dream of Jeannie.*

Flaming Star

Elvis in *Flaming Star*. With a respected director, Don Siegal, and a cast of notable actors, *Flaming Star* was the serious movie that Elvis had been wanting to make for some time. Although a version with four songs was also shot, the final release only had two—which greatly disappointed some fans.

Rough and tumble

Opposite: Although Elvis made it through the rough and tumble of filming without accident, he broke his finger while playing touch football between takes.

Right: Chief Wah-Nee-Ota inducts Elvis into the Los Angeles Indian Tribal Council in recognition of his role in *Flaming Star*.

Below: Elvis with the Jordanaires recording a song for the soundtrack of one of his movies.

CHAPTER FOUR

Are You Lonesome Tonight?

During 1961 Elvis performed live only three times—two concerts at the Ellis Auditorium in Memphis and a charity event for the USS *Arizona* at Bloch Arena at Pearl Harbor, Hawaii. The live appearances had become a danger to all concerned—he had to arrive and leave in the greatest secrecy as the fans behaved so wildly in their attempts to reach him that there was a real risk that someone would soon get hurt. Elvis was also now concentrating on his movie career, and since he went on to make three pictures a year for most of the rest of the 1960s there was little time left for concert tours.

The overall quality of Elvis's movies has sometimes been criticized, particularly since at the beginning of his Hollywood career several of his directors and fellow actors thought he was capable of even greater things. However, a great many of his movies were not only highly successful at the box office but were also well received by movie critics. In common with many other musical and comedy stars, almost all his movies were specifically written as a vehicle for their leading man—feel-good stories with lots of songs worked into the script. Elvis himself knew that he could also do darker and more complex roles, given

the chance—he said several times in interviews that he wanted to become a serious actor and do dramatic parts. Some people blamed the Colonel for Elvis's failure to widen the range of roles he played, feeling that the desire to make ever more money made the Colonel short-sighted with regard to wider issues. His tireless negotiating for higher fees was certainly a factor in encouraging the studios to play safe and go for the tried and tested to protect their investment. *Flaming Star* and *Wild in the Country* had taken a different line and moved away from singing but they did less well at the box office. On the other hand, *Blue Hawaii*, a lightweight musical comedy built round an exotic location, was a massive hit. Several of the later movies were therefore made to a similar formula. Elvis knew that they were not all that he wanted to do, that he had other ambitions to fulfil, but no one could deny that they were attracting large audiences and making money. Although he was offered some interesting and controversial roles, the Colonel turned them down, both because they did not fit the formula he had established and because they would not have been so lucrative.

Meanwhile, Elvis's personal life was as complicated as ever. At the beginning of the 1960s he was still dating Anita, but seeing other girls whenever she was not around—the

Memphis Mafia were always there to cover for him. He had also remained in touch with Priscilla in Germany, and in March 1962 he began to talk to her parents about the possibility of her coming over to America. Understandably they were not sure about the idea, but he arranged for her to stay "officially" with friends. Priscilla was still only 17, and Elvis himself was conscious of the potential problems if the press found out he was seeing such a young girl. Priscilla finally arrived in Los Angeles and after a few days they left to see Las Vegas, but all too soon she had to return. Despite all their precautions, Anita knew what was happening and decided it was time to move on.

Priscilla returned a few months later, to spend Christmas with Elvis at Graceland. Again the time seemed too short, so Elvis came up with the idea that she should stay in America and finish her schooling at a local Catholic school. Her parents refused to consider it at first, but eventually they gave in. Priscilla moved in with Dee and Vernon and was enrolled in the Immaculate Conception High School, but since Elvis was away in Hollywood working on yet another movie, she soon moved into Graceland. When he was at home they did everything together and he began to mold her into his perfect woman, but she found it difficult to get used to having so many people around. In Germany only a couple of his cronies had been with him, so they had often had time alone together. Now there always seemed to be a crowd of people and she often felt out of place amongst the Memphis Mafia and their older wives and girlfriends.

Things soon became even more complicated. The costar of Elvis's next movie was Ann-Margret, and she and Elvis quickly realized that they were kindred spirits. Unlike Priscilla, who was shy and terrified of putting a foot wrong with Elvis's entourage, Ann-Margret was full of energy and mischief and soon came to be regarded as one of the boys. Several people commented that they had never seen Elvis so happy, and word began to leak into the papers that she and Elvis were an item. It came to a head when Ann-Margret went to London for the royal première of her previous movie and the British press reported that she had talked of marrying Elvis. The US papers quickly picked up the story; Priscilla was furious and upset—and so was Elvis. He assured the press that if he planned to marry they would hear about it from him, and to Priscilla he denied everything and told her she was the only woman for him. Ann-Margret later refuted the claims that she had said anything but, although she and Elvis remained in contact and continued to see each other in secret, from then on they began to drift apart.

By 1964 The Beatles had hit America and were blasting through the charts, but Elvis had not had a major hit since "Return to Sender" in 1962. He had somehow lost his direction and he felt increasingly unhappy, lonely, and empty. At this point he met hairdresser Larry Geller, who introduced him to spirituality and the search for self-knowledge. Most of those around him did not share his interest and resented the newcomer, but Elvis became immersed in his new way of life and spent as much time as possible studying over the next couple of years. Despite this, he was also still relying heavily on amphetamines—as were most members of the Memphis Mafia. It all came to a head when he missed the start of filming on his new picture, Clambake, saying he was sick. The Colonel demanded a doctor's certificate and although a local doctor, Dr. Nichopoulos, provided one, the Colonel decided things had gone far enough. Elvis was not focusing on business—and since the movies were currently not making as much money as they had, this was no time for "his boy" to become unreliable. The Colonel fired some of the entourage and made sure Geller was gradually excluded, after which Elvis soon began to return to his old interests.

There was now also Elvis's forthcoming wedding to prepare for. Priscilla had been living at Graceland for more than three years and both she and her father—and the Colonel—had been dropping heavy hints to Elvis about fulfilling his commitments. They finally became engaged at Christmas 1966, and the wedding was set for May 1 1967, in Las Vegas. The ceremony itself was private—even the Memphis Mafia and their wives and girlfriends were excluded, although they were invited to the reception. Afterwards the newlyweds went back to Palm Springs and then on to the Flying Circle G in Mississippi, the ranch that Elvis had bought earlier that year. Although several members of the entourage came with them, Priscilla later said it was an idyllic time in which their privacy was respected and she was able to enjoy looking after her new husband herself. At the end of the month they returned to Graceland and had another big reception for those who had missed the first. Within a few weeks, Priscilla realized she was pregnant. At first she was upset, because for the first time she had been feeling a real part of Elvis's life in America and now everything would inevitably change, but Elvis was delighted at the prospect of becoming a father. After Lisa Marie Presley was born on February 1, 1968, Elvis announced that he was the happiest man in the world.

Although his personal life seemed to have settled down, the problems in Elvis's career now came to a head. The fans were less devoted to seeing Elvis in every movie he made, and although a gospel album, *How Great Thou Art*, was selling steadily, his other records were not doing that well. The songs being supplied for movie soundtracks were often so formulaic that even the Colonel was moved to protest. Unfortunately, much of the reason for that went back to the old arrangements he himself had set up for writers requiring them to forgo part of their royalty before Elvis would record their song. Understandably, the best material was now no longer offered to him.

A change of direction was clearly needed and Elvis was ready to make it. The Colonel had arranged for him to appear in a TV special, which was to be broadcast just before Christmas 1968. It was to be recorded before a live audience—the first time Elvis had sung on stage for seven years. The Colonel wanted "his boy" to sing a straightforward selection of Christmas songs, but NBC producer Bob Finkel convinced Elvis to go for a radical change of image. Director Steve Binder put together a show that featured Elvis in black leather belting out his rock 'n' roll hits, and finished with a brand new song, "If I Can Dream." It was a total triumph. Everyone who had forgotten what Elvis was capable of and hearing him sing the old hits with an exciting new freshness was a revelation to many.

Elvis himself was now determined to return to touring. From his new position of strength, the Colonel

arranged a four-week booking at the brand-new International Hotel that was due to open in Las Vegas that July. It was certainly a gamble: Elvis's only previous appearance in Las Vegas had been a disaster; the room he was being expected to fill had a capacity almost twice those that current major headliners played; and it would all take place in a full glare of publicity. Meanwhile, some changes had also been made in terms of how the records were recorded. The last few studio sessions in Nashville had been fairly disastrous, with only the minimum usable material laid down. Elvis was persuaded to try American, a small new studio in Memphis that had produced a string of hits under the direction of its principal owner, Chips Moman. The sessions were an unqualified success and Elvis recorded some of his best material to date, with the first single released, "In the Ghetto," giving him a major hit and another gold record.

The opening night in Las Vegas on July 31, 1969, was the first time Elvis had performed a full concert in public for more than eight years. He was visibly nervous beforehand, but when he came out on stage and launched into his first number, his uninhibited love for the music combined with his instinctive sense of what the audience wanted created a sensational show. Those watching exploded with excitement and even the critics spoke of a mesmerizing performance. By the end of the run his female fans were throwing underwear onto the stage, just like in the old days. The hotel management were quick to pick up their option on further shows, booking Elvis to appear twice a year for the next five years.

Unfortunately, while Elvis was now riding high in his career, his personal life was not going so well; although outwardly they appeared the perfect couple, Elvis and Priscilla were already having problems. After Lisa Marie was born, Elvis had made it plain to Priscilla that he was no longer physically attracted to her. Unhappy and unfulfilled, Priscilla had begun an affair with her dance instructor. No one dared tell Elvis—but it was only a matter of time before the marriage would begin to fall apart.

Wild in the Country

Opposite and above: Elvis with Hope Lange in *Wild in the Country*, in which he played Glenn Tyler, who serves time in a juvenile institution and then attempts to sort out his life. Although there were originally no songs in the movie, several were added after it was noted that the previous serious movie, *Flaming Star*, was not doing as well at the box office.

Left: In *Blue Hawaii*, Elvis played Chad Gates, the son of a wealthy plantation owner who disappears to the beach to play music with his native Hawaiian friends—and ends up in jail!

Blue Hawaii

Opposite: Fans cluster around a lei-clad Elvis as he stands in Los Angeles airport before flying to Hawaii to star in *Blue Hawaii*. He was also scheduled to make several benefit appearances during his three-week stay on the island.

Above: In a scene from the movie, Guy Lee as Ping Pong tries to spray water at Roland Winters as Fred Gates, Elvis, Angela Lansbury as Sarah Lee Gates, and John Archer as Fred Kelman.

The soundtrack of *Blue Hawaii* featured 14 other numbers as well as "Can't Help Falling in Love." The music ranged across several musical styles. There were extensive shots of the Hawaiian scenery, with shooting at Waikiki Beach, Hanauma Bay, and Ala Moana Park.

Right: Elvis and the Colonel on the set of *Blue Hawaii*.

Dreading deep water…

Opposite: Joan Blackman with Elvis on the beach. During the filming of *Blue Hawaii*, Elvis revealed that he was apprehensive in deep water. Director Norman Taurog gave him the option of doing scenes on the beach instead, but Elvis bravely faced his fear and most of them were shot in or on the ocean, as originally called for in the script. Elvis made several movies in Hawaii, including *Blue Hawaii* (1961), *Girls! Girls! Girls!* (1962), and *Paradise Hawaiian Style* (1965). "Can't Help Falling in Love," from the soundtrack of *Blue Hawaii*, was released as a single in October 1961 and went on to become a massive hit that year.

Above: Angela Lansbury was cast as Elvis's mother—although she was only 35 at the time.

Follow That Dream!

Above: *Blue Hawaii* was released not long before Christmas 1961, and quickly turned a profit. It grossed almost $5 million and the soundtrack album became the fastest-selling LP of that year. In 1962, United Artists released *Follow That Dream*. Here Elvis and costar Joanne Moore enjoy a little dalliance on the beach in a scene from the movie. The title song from the movie was released in April 1962 and went on to become a big hit.

Opposite above: Elvis got lost on his way to the wedding of his secretary, Pat Boyd, to one of the Memphis Mafia, Bobby West, and so he missed the ceremony. He arrived just in time for the reception.

Kid Galahad

Right: In *Kid Galahad*, Elvis played a gallant boxer—although the bruises are the work of the studio makeup department. He was unhappy about his appearance because his weight had recently shot up, and he did not enjoy making the movie. One bright spot was taking boxing lessons from former welterweight champion Mushy Callahan, for whom Elvis felt deep respect. He tried to impress costar Charles Bronson, who was playing his trainer in the movie, but the veteran actor had little time for him.

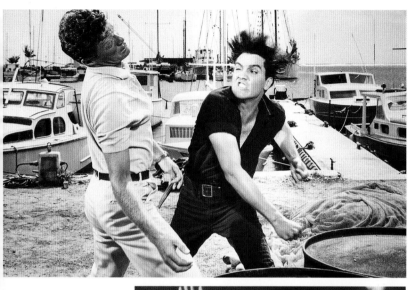

1962: Return to Sender

Above: In a fit of anger, Elvis slugs Jeremy
Slate, who has tried to steal his girl. *Girls!*
Girls! Girls! was shot in Hawaii. Otis Blackwell's
"Return to Sender," which featured in the
movie, was released as a single in October
1962.

Right: The storyline of *Fun in Acapulco* had
Elvis as a former trapeze artist, who develops
a phobia after his partner is severely injured.
He gets a job as a lifeguard in a luxurious
Mexican resort instead, and falls in love with
the hotel's social director, played by Ursula
Andress. Exteriors were shot on location in
Mexico, but Elvis stayed on the Paramount
lot in Hollywood. *Fun in Acapulco* went on to
become the top-grossing movie of 1963.

Opposite: Elvis in *Kid Galahad*.

Summer of 1962

Above: Elvis and his entourage arrive in Seattle, accompanied by police officers. They had come to the city for location filming for *It Happened at the World's Fair*—the 1962 World's Fair was being held there at the time.

Opposite: Elvis gets a manicure on Seattle's monorail. He and the guys were prone to elaborate jokes to liven up the boredom of filming. One of their favorites was to call for room service after having removed all the furniture from the room—then to have it all back in place by the time the manager arrived.

Following pages: Joan O'Brien and Elvis in a scene from *It Happened at the World's Fair*.

1963: Viva Las Vegas

Opposite, left, and following pages: Ann-Margret and Elvis during filming of *Viva Las Vegas* for MGM in 1963. Ann-Margret was known as the "female Elvis Presley" because of her sensual performing style, and rumors quickly began circulating that the two stars were having an affair. This time the rumors were true—despite the fact that Priscilla was already quietly living at Graceland. Because of the sexual chemistry between the two stars, the musical numbers in the movie vibrate with a sensual passion not found in Elvis's other movies.

Below: Elvis and Ann-Margret shared a love of motorcycles—much to the consternation of production staff, since an accident involving either of them could have delayed filming for many weeks.

Making friends

Opposite: Even after their romance cooled, Elvis and Ann-Margret stayed close friends—right up to the end of his life—and he always sent flowers to her on opening nights.

Above: During a break in the filming of their respective movies, Jim Brown drops in on Elvis for a chat. Elvis had long been an admirer of the other actor's work and had wanted to meet him for some time. Elvis was currently filming *Roustabout*, in which he played a carnival hand with a knack for getting into trouble. Barbara Stanwyck was the boss and the two stars initially did not get on. Later they became friends and Elvis said the experience of working with her had inspired him to become a better actor.

March 1964: Filming for Roustabout

Opposite and right: Barbara Stanwyck pictured with Elvis. *Roustabout* was set against the background of a small American carnival—a life that the Colonel certainly knew inside out. He had suggested the original idea back in 1961, and as the script developed he came up with many pieces of "carny" business to include in the story. Part of the action for *Roustabout* was filmed on location, at Thousand Oaks just northwest of Los Angeles and at the Hidden Valley Ranch in California. Elvis insisted on doing a fight sequence himself, and was hit on the head. He needed four stitches but, since the script called for him to be ridden off the road on his motorcycle, the genuine injury was used and filming continued.

Below: As well as Barbara Stanwyck, the movie also costarred Joan Freeman as the girl who fights Elvis all the way, but who eventually falls in love with him. The Stanwyck part was originally offered to Mae West, but she turned it down.

Taking on the bad guys

Opposite: *Tickle Me* was Elvis's first picture for Allied Artists. His salary of $750,000 was half the budget, and he also had a 50 percent share of the profits. Allied Artists was in financial trouble and the Colonel offered to let them out of their agreement, but studio head Steve Broidy refused. Director Norman Taurog, on his fifth Presley movie, was asked to try to bring *Tickle Me* in under budget— both to help Allied Artists and to ensure the movie was completed. Since he was a fast and efficient worker, who got on well with Elvis, he managed to come in under what was already a tight costing.

Right: Enjoying a joke with one of his costars on the set of *Tickle Me*. Away from the cameras, Elvis had found a much more serious interest. He had recently met Larry Geller, a hairdresser who had introduced him to alternative religions.

Below: Elvis sings in *Tickle Me*.

Tickle Me

In *Tickle Me*, Elvis played an unemployed rodeo star, who accepts a job at a health farm. He helps one of the girls escape from the clutches of villains, who are looking for treasure. The health farm setting ensured that there was plenty of opportunity to feature scantily-clad starlets.

Tickle Me saved Allied Artists from going under, its gross only coming in behind that of *55 Days in Peking* and *El Cid* in the company's history. It also made the usual profit for Elvis and the Colonel.

Selecting a soundtrack

Elvis in *Tickle Me*. One way in which
the Colonel maximized profits from
Tickle Me was to arrange with Allied
that the movie soundtrack would
only utilize songs already recorded
by Elvis—which he guaranteed
would not have appeared on
a single or EP. In this way they
could avoid the costs of recording
original soundtrack material, while
at the same time still being able to
release a soundtrack record.

Many of the songs featured in
Elvis's movies are very good—there
is "Return to Sender" from *Girls!
Girls! Girls!*, "Wolf Call" from *Girl
Happy* and "Can't Help Falling in
Love" from *Blue Hawaii*.

Paradise regained in 1965

Above: Elvis in *Paradise, Hawaiian Style*. He had always enjoyed being in Hawaii before, but this time reporters noted that he seemed rather depressed. Nevertheless, he threw himself into the making of the movie, in which he sang some traditional Hawaiian folk songs. Elvis had not had a song in the charts for a while, but now "Crying in the Chapel," which had been recorded some time before and released in April 1965, was a top ten hit.

Opposite: Elvis makes a charity donation, received by comedian Danny Thomas.

Following pages: A still from *Spinout*, which was released in November 1966.

Action hero

Opposite: The typical Presley hero was always a man of action, often with an interesting or unusual job—who could also sing. In *Spinout*, a movie for MGM again directed by Norman Taurog, he was a racing driver. The 1929 Duesenberg in which he is supposed to enter the Santa Fe Road Race was a priceless classic car.

Right: *Harum Scarum* was a light-hearted movie, set in the desert, produced by Sam Katzman and directed by Gene Nelson. The costumes were designed to make Elvis look like a modern Rudolf Valentino.

Above: While Elvis was making *Frankie and Johnnie* for United Artists, he was deeply absorbed by studies of religion, philosophy, and the occult. Costar Donna Douglas was both religious and spiritual, and Elvis spent hours with her discussing the books they had each read. He was rather overweight during filming, but his costumes were cleverly cut to hide it.

Back-to-back filming

Above: Elvis in a scene from *Clambake*. He was now filming for much of the year—*Easy Come, Easy Go* had begun shooting just three weeks after *Double Trouble* had finished, although there was then a three-month break before *Clambake* began.

Opposite: The producers of Elvis's movies always kept an eye on what was going on in popular culture. When European discotheques were all the rage, Elvis appeared in *Double Trouble*, which was set in the discotheques of London and Amsterdam. Elvis did not go on location abroad to film—all his scenes were shot in Hollywood. During the course of the eight-week shooting schedule, Elvis presented his leading lady, Annette Day, with a blue and white Mustang,

Clambake

Opposite: Elvis in a publicity still for *Clambake*, in which he played the son of a rich man who agrees to trade places with a water skiing instructor in order to try to be accepted for himself rather than be popular because of his father's money.

Right: In this publicity photograph Elvis looks handsome and well, but by the late 1960s his health was beginning to be adversely affected by his lifestyle.

1967: Priscilla and Elvis say "I do"

Opposite, above, and following pages: On May 1, 1967, Elvis and Priscilla Beaulieu are married by Nevada Supreme Court Justice David Zenoff, in a private ceremony held in a suite in the English-Tudor-style Aladdin Hotel in Las Vegas. After the eight-minute ceremony was over, a press conference was held in the Aladdin Room of the hotel. Priscilla showed off her three-carat diamond ring and the happy couple kissed for the benefit of photographers. Priscilla's father told the newsmen that he had known from the beginning that the two of them would marry one day. Priscilla said later that they had both been so nervous before the ceremony that neither of them had slept the previous night.

Celebrating in style

Right: There were over one hundred people at the reception, eating a buffet banquet while a string trio played romantic ballads—including some of the groom's hits. However, most members of the Memphis Mafia had been excluded from the actual ceremony—lack of space in the suite was cited as the reason—and were invited to the reception only. It caused some resentment, and marked the beginning of disaffection in the Mafia ranks.

Man and wife

Opposite and left: The happy couple returned to Palm Springs after the reception, but three days later left for Memphis and on to the Circle G Ranch. Although most of the Memphis Mafia came with them, living on the ranch without the household staff gave Priscilla a chance to "play house" and look after her new husband herself. At the end of the month, they held another wedding ceremony at Graceland—a less formal affair that included the entire Graceland staff and all Elvis's uncles, aunts, and cousins, as well as his doctor, dentist, painter, horse trainer, and electrician.

Speedway

In *Speedway*, Elvis played a racing driver for the third time and the movie was director Norman Taurog's eighth Presley picture. Many of the Memphis Mafia had small roles in the film—and even Taurog's small granddaughter had a part. Elvis's costar and love-interest in *Speedway* was Nancy Sinatra, and rumors circulated in the press that the two of them were having an affair in real life. They had been linked romantically several times previously but Elvis just liked to flirt with any available woman.

Nancy and Elvis

Above: Despite all the rumors, after Lisa Marie was born it was Nancy Sinatra who held a baby shower for Priscilla.

When asked by a journalist what kind of part he played in *Speedway*, Elvis answered, "I'm kinduva singin' millionaire-playboy-race driver, sir." The journalist went on to ask if Elvis had ever played such a part before, and he replied, "Only about 25 times, sir."

Proud parents

Right: On February 1, 1968, Priscilla gave birth to a baby girl. After the birth of his daughter, Elvis told everyone that he was the happiest man in the world. He had often told people over the years that if he had a daughter he would name her Gladys after his mother, but they had finally selected the name Lisa Marie. Both denied there was any significance in either name—although the Colonel's wife was called Marie.

Opposite and below: Priscilla left the Baptist Memorial Hospital in Memphis four days after the birth of Lisa Marie, escorted by Elvis, Vernon, and a host of others.

Fun on location in 1967

Above: In *Stay Away, Joe*, Elvis's character was an Indian rodeo rider, Joe Whitecloud, and the storyline pitted Indian ingenuity against government bureaucracy. There were originally only three songs—another was added later. *Stay Away, Joe* had a good cast, with veteran actors Burgess Meredith, Thomas Gomez, and Katy Jurado. They all had fun on location—even the Colonel joined in, making a promotional calendar out of a picture of himself taken by the pool with a snarling face and several days' growth of beard.

Opposite: A publicity picture of a more mature Elvis, taken in 1968.

1968: Live a Little, Love a Little

Elvis in *Live a Little, Love a Little*, a comedy that was based on a popular novel by Dan Greenburg, *Kiss My Firm but Pliant Lips*. Again the director was Norman Taurog and the screenplay included only four songs. *Live a Little, Love a Little* was released in October 1968.

Elvis tires of moviemaking

Opposite: In *Live a Little, Love a Little*, Elvis played a successful photographer. By the late 1960s Elvis wanted a rest from making movies but, because of the Colonel's habit of negotiating block contracts, he was contractually obliged to make several more.

Right: In his last few movies, Elvis made a break from the kind of things he had done before. *Charro!* was a hard-hitting western, in which the fans were treated to a bearded and rugged Elvis.

Below: Elvis and Priscilla visit Tom Jones backstage at his show in the Flamingo Hotel in Las Vegas. Tom Jones was often compared to an early Elvis in style—and in his appeal to the female fans.

Mutual respect

Elvis and Priscilla inspect Tom Jones's
watch backstage in Las Vegas. Elvis
had first met Tom Jones in Los Angeles
in 1965 and they became friends,
regarding each other with mutual
respect. Elvis sometimes sang Jones's
song "Delilah" backstage before
performances to warm up his voice.

The Trouble with Girls in 1968

Above and opposite: *The Trouble With Girls* was set in the 1920s, with Elvis as the manager of a chautauqua—a traveling college that brought culture to rural areas and isolated villages. Elvis doesn't appear until about one-third of the way into the picture but his character is important in holding together the various sub-plots in the movie.

Left: A publicity shot for the forthcoming *Comeback Special* gives little idea of the new-look Elvis that is about to burst onto the TV screen.

Christmas 1968: Back to his roots

A leather-clad Elvis shows how it used to be, in the *Comeback Special* aired on NBC at Christmas. The Colonel had originally wanted him merely to sing a few Christmas songs, but NBC producer Steve Binder persuaded him to go back to his roots. He challenged Elvis to walk down the street and see if he was recognized by young people. Elvis was reluctant, since he had not been out without an escort for some years, but he decided to try. When no-one recognized him, he agreed that his career needed a major boost.

A huge success

Elvis pictured during the *Comeback Special*. The show opened with Elvis singing "Guitar Man" against a backdrop reminiscent of *Jailhouse Rock* (left) and ended with a rendition of "If I Can Dream" (opposite). The show was watched by millions of Americans, giving CBS its highest ratings of the year.

A Change of Habit

Opposite and below: In *A Change of Habit* Elvis played a doctor working in a ghetto who falls in love with the character played by Mary Tyler Moore, unaware that she is a nun.

Right: Elvis as Dr Carpenter in *A Change of Habit*. The movie, Elvis's thirty-first, was to be his last feature film. The success of the *Comeback Special* had relaunched his singing career and, after ten years of making movies, Elvis was keen to change direction.

   While Elvis's career was going from strength to strength Priscilla was becoming dissatisfied with their marriage. As soon as he began performing again, Elvis was spending long periods of time away from home, leaving Priscilla and Lisa Marie alone. The pace of the tours meant it was difficult for wives and families to travel with the group, so Elvis himself had instigated a strict no-wives rule. To make up for his long absences, Elvis showered both Lisa Marie and Priscilla with expensive presents on both birthdays and Christmas.

Standing ovation for live performance

Elvis at a press conference following the opening night of the first of the Las Vegas shows in summer 1969. Newsmen from all over the world had gathered to see him perform and Elvis told them "I'm really glad to be back in front of a live audience. I don't think I have ever been more excited than I was tonight." The show had been the first time he had performed in public for more than eight years, and he had received four standing ovations.

"Suspicious Minds" was released the following September—it went on to become a top ten single and one of Elvis's signature tunes. In 1969, Elvis also had several other top ten hits—including "Don't Cry Daddy" and "In the Ghetto."

CHAPTER FIVE

Return to Sender

Even at the beginning of the 1970s, it was apparent to most people that Elvis's behavior was becoming increasingly erratic, not only in private but also on stage. What was not so well known was that this was due to the quantity and mixture of prescription drugs he was taking; they not only caused mood swings, but also increased his paranoia—especially after there were threats to kill or kidnap him during a show. Not long afterward, he was sworn in as a special deputy so he could carry a hand-gun, and this soon led to an obsession with collecting police badges and firearms. After meeting voice-over artist Paul Frees and learning that he worked as an undercover narcotics agent—complete with an official Bureau of Narcotics and Dangerous Drugs badge—Elvis was determined to get a BNDD badge for himself. Having failed to get one from the Bureau, Elvis simply asked President Nixon for one instead, not only getting in to see the then US President at the White House, but also securing the sought-after badge.

Elvis and Priscilla were drifting apart. Elvis carried on much as he had always done; there were women virtually on tap when he needed the company, and often it was indeed just that—for company. Many women said later that when they spent the night with him, nothing happened except perhaps a little kissing—he just didn't want to sleep alone. However, there were also several more prolonged affairs. The drugs he was taking often made him difficult to deal with and most women soon tired of a role that was always on his terms, and often seemed to be that of mother rather than lover.

By the end of 1971, Priscilla had developed an interest in karate … and in martial arts expert Mike Stone. After taking Lisa Marie to spend Christmas at Graceland, she told Elvis that she no longer loved him, and returned to Hollywood before the New Year. Two months later she told him about Mike Stone. Elvis was furious that she preferred another man to him, even though he had never been faithful to her, and soon began to date former beauty queen Linda Thompson, who moved into Graceland later that year.

After the success of his recent Las Vegas show, Elvis had embarked on a tour of America, breaking box office records wherever he went; he also appeared regularly for long "residency" bookings in Las Vegas and at nearby Lake Tahoe. From 1969 to 1977 he played a total of almost 1,100 concerts despite his failing health toward the end of that time. Although, at the start, he obviously enjoyed being back on the stage, toward the

Opposite: Elvis in concert during the mid 1970s.

end he was really just going through the motions and even the most ardent fans were often disappointed. Many people wondered why he continued with such a punishing schedule, but it was principally for the money.

Elvis had established a costly lifestyle, with large numbers of hangers-on as well as family members relying on him for a living. He was also outrageously generous—not only to people he knew well but also to perfect strangers. He often gave away cars, expensive jewelery and money, and even bought houses for several of his associates. And it was not only Elvis's own lifestyle that had to be maintained. The Colonel had once had a reputation for never spending his own money; he and his wife lived at the William Morris Agency's expense in a house in Palm Springs and he made sure that everyone contributed to the expense of his staff and office space. However, once Elvis had started to appear regularly at Las Vegas, the Colonel developed a passion for gambling and regularly lost at least $1 million a year at the roulette wheel. Many of his close associates became concerned, but found themselves unable to do anything to stop what was happening. Ironically, before they went to Vegas, the Colonel had warned some of the members of the Memphis Mafia not to get hooked on gambling and now he had fallen into the trap himself.

Despite his problems, the Colonel was not one to neglect business and he soon had another mega-deal organized. *Elvis: Aloha From Hawaii* was a concert on a grand scale that would be broadcast round the world by satellite. Even Elvis was caught up in the excitement of the event, losing some weight for the show and picking out songs that he had not recorded before. Linda Thompson seemed good for him, her sunny personality lifted his mood and she was happy to be with him constantly, attending to his every need. It almost seemed as if Elvis might have turned a corner, as if from now on things would improve.

Unfortunately, this was just an illusion. The Colonel could not understand why Elvis was becoming so irresponsible, and they were soon no longer communicating properly. Things came to a head in Las Vegas when Elvis made derogatory comments on-stage about the management of the Hilton hotel, which now owned the former International. The Colonel was livid and they had a furious row, with Elvis sacking the Colonel just as he quit. They did not speak to each other for several weeks afterward.

The cocktail of drugs he was taking also made Elvis so ill that he missed several shows and, later in the year at Lake Tahoe, the same thing happened again. In an attempt to stop what was happening, a private detective was hired to find out the source of Elvis's drug supplies. Three doctors and a dentist were identified, but little further action was taken. Those around him seemed to believe that Elvis would pull through on his own, just as he had dropped other things when they ceased to interest him.

In October 1973, Elvis's divorce from Priscilla was finalized. A few days later he was admitted to hospital and the papers reported he had collapsed because he was so upset about the end of his marriage. The reality was that he had suffered a serious reaction to the drugs he was taking. His doctor, George Nichopoulos, brought in a team of specialists, who stabilized his condition and then began an investigation into just what had caused the problem. Finally they discovered that Elvis was getting almost daily doses of pethidine, a painkiller, and was seriously addicted. He was also regularly taking tranquillizers, cortisone, and sleeping pills, as well as adopting various quick-fix diets whenever he needed to lose weight in a hurry. All this had done him considerable physical damage. After quietly undergoing a drug withdrawal program in hospital, Elvis was nursed back to health. His room at Graceland was searched and all drugs removed before he returned home, where he spent the next couple of months recuperating. His collapse had scared him so much that, for a while at least, he was a good patient, and Dr. Nichopoulos visited him on almost a daily basis to try to moderate his diet and to supervise his medication.

When he returned to Las Vegas towards the end of January 1974, Elvis was slimmer and fitter than he had been for some years. A few weeks after the end of that Vegas season, he began touring again, and this time Dr. Nichopoulos came with him. Elvis was still taking an assortment of painkillers, tranquillizers, and sleeping pills, but Dr. Nichopoulos had worked out a daily program to keep things on an even keel, adding multivitamins and substituting placebos for some of the drugs when he thought Elvis didn't really need them. Although, on the surface, things had stabilized, on stage Elvis was still behaving in an eccentric way.

The music had become rather mundane, he no longer sang with any discernible emotion and he often stopped singing and addressed the audience on any subject that happened to take his fancy, including his personal life, karate, and religion.

Meanwhile, sales of his new record releases were down. His last few recording sessions had generated little suitable material—perhaps due to his health problems, or perhaps just because of tiredness after years of almost continuous performing. Since RCA had purchased all rights to Elvis's back catalogue from the Colonel for $5.4 million in 1973, it now began to concentrate on releasing a series of records containing his old material; sales of these far outstripped those of Elvis's current releases and were not liable for royalties.

Elvis's commitment to his new health regime did not last long. By the end of 1974 he had put on weight again and was severely depressed. He spent his 40th birthday in seclusion and, at the end of January, was rushed back into hospital and treated again to get his use of drugs back under control. While he was there, his father Vernon had a heart attack and joined him in the same hospital. After leaving hospital, Elvis stayed at Graceland to rest and lose more weight. Again, his resolution did not last long and, within a few months, he was gaining weight and finding the drugs he wanted despite all attempts to stop him. During

concerts he often appeared exhausted, but the fans still loved him. In August, several shows in Las Vegas had to be canceled due to Elvis's poor health, and he was re-admitted to hospital. By now, Linda Thompson had realized that she would never be able to save Elvis from himself, and with great reluctance she began to make a life away from him.

With canceled engagements, a restricted touring schedule, and no new record releases, there wasn't so much money coming in. Vernon persuaded Elvis that they needed to cut expenses and three members of the Memphis Mafia were fired—Red and Sonny West and Dave Hebler. Soon afterward, the three of them got together with journalist Steve Dunleavy to write a book exposing what life had been like with Elvis. He was deeply upset at what he saw as a betrayal, and also worried about what his fans would think of some of the more lurid revelations.

With his entourage cut back to almost nothing, and Linda Thompson pursuing her own career, Elvis was feeling abandoned and alone. At this point he was introduced to Ginger Alden, a 20-year-old former beauty queen. Although many believed that she never really loved Elvis, he pursued her avidly, buying her cars and expensive presents and soon asked her to marry him. She accompanied him on several tours and her presence seemed to give him a new lease of life for a short while.

At the end of July 1977, Lisa Marie came to Graceland for a two-week visit. Elvis seemed in a good mood for most of the time, although he was slightly edgy about his next tour. On August 15 he had a couple of teeth filled and later played some racquetball, as usual settling down to try and sleep in the early hours of the morning. Despite three doses of medication he was unable to settle, and told Ginger that he would go to the bathroom to read. She awoke early in the afternoon of the 16th to find that she was still alone in bed, and went to investigate. She found Elvis lying on the floor of his bathroom, but she was too late. The King of rock 'n' roll was dead.

Elvis on tour

Opposite and right: A shot from the documentary *That's The Way It Is*. Those involved in making the film were deeply involved in their subject. They approached Elvis in concert as if he were a folk hero on a mythic journey. In addition, they had the latest mobile cameras and equipment, which brought movement and spontaneity to the filming.

As well as shots of Elvis performing, the filmmakers— Bob Abel and Pierre Adidge—included backstage material, shots of past glories, and candid moments. The final film is one of the classic records of Elvis's career.

At the beginning, Abel had told Elvis, "I want to shoot the real you… but you've got to be open with me. If I feel that you're posing or doing something, I'll just turn the camera off." Elvis appreciated his honesty, and from then on was committed to the project.

Below: When Elvis began appearing in Las Vegas regularly during the 1970s, there was no doubt that he was a major star. The Hilton Hotel chain had taken over the International in June the previous year and before the deal was even signed they were anxious to make sure that Vegas's premier attraction would continue to appear in their hotel.

That's The Way It Is

Above: The premiere of *Elvis: That's The Way It Is* was in November 1970. Elvis is seen playing a guitar during one of the scenes, and he is obviously not as fit, healthy and vibrantly alive as he had appeared in the *Comeback Special* just two years earlier.

Meeting the President

Above: After Elvis wrote to President Nixon, offering to help stamp out drugs, he was invited to the White House to meet the President. After Nixon agreed to give Elvis a coveted BNDD badge, Elvis stepped forward and hugged him—taking both the President and his aide off guard.

Right: Elvis in *That's the Way It Is*. The idea for the famous jumpsuits apparently came from Priscilla, who suggested Elvis should wear them on stage because they would be more comfortable and allow him to move freely.

The best Elvis film ever

Opposite and above: *Elvis: That's The Way It Is* was filmed on tour and covered several concerts. Although now it appears rather dated, it is still an atmospheric record of a star in concert. Even the Colonel was won over by Abel and Adidge, telling them to "Go out there and make the best Elvis film ever." And that's more or less what they did.

First time at Madison Square Garden

Above: At a press conference in New York, where he was appearing for the first time at Madison Square Garden, Elvis soon won over the jaded newsmen. When asked how he thought he had managed to outlast every other performer from his generation, he quickly quipped, "I take vitamin E."

Right: Although appearing in New York had been a bit of a gamble, all four performances at Madison Square Garden were sold out—a total of 80,000 tickets.

Opposite: Elvis greets Governor George C. Wallace in Montgomery, Alabama, when he performed there at the Garrett Coliseum. Governor Wallace and his family were among the audience of more than 11,000 who came to see the show.

Hard to live up to the image
At the press conference, Elvis was accompanied by both the Colonel and his father (opposite below).
A reporter asked Elvis if he was happy with his image, but Elvis pointed out that the image was one
thing, but a human being was another. He then added, "It's very hard to live up to an image."

Putting on the style in Vegas

The jumpsuits that Elvis wore in Las Vegas have become a symbol that represent this stage of his career. Most of them were designed by tailor Bill Belew, and they became increasingly elaborate. Sometimes they incorporated a cape—either waist or floor-length—and they were decorated with real gemstones and semiprecious jewels. The symbols used on some of the later costumes were of special significance to Elvis—eagles, karate symbols, tigers, peacocks, and the fans often gave these outfits special names.

Spectacular success

Above: At a press conference in Las Vegas, Elvis announced that he would soon be going on a worldwide concert tour.

Opposite: The Colonel put together a new project, which was massive in both scale and ambition. *Aloha From Hawaii* was a television special, with Elvis's performance beamed live via satellite to countries all over the world. It was also taped for re-transmission to most of the remaining countries a few days later. Elvis looked slim, fit, and handsome again. The project was a spectacular success.

Aloha

Elvis wearing the American Eagle jumpsuit, designed by Bill Belew, during *Aloha From Hawaii*. Always generous, Elvis had caused a problem by giving away the jewel-encrusted belt for the costume to *Hawaii Five-0* actor Jack Lord shortly after his arrival in Hawaii and a new belt had to be created. At the end of the show Elvis also gave away his cape, throwing it into the audience.

Final performances

Elvis increasingly had a problem controlling his weight. His poor diet certainly didn't help, but the additional weight was also due to lack of exercise. He was taking a dangerous combination of prescription drugs and he was hospitalized several times. Many of those close to him tried to cut his drug intake, but Elvis was used to getting his own way. Despite his bloated appearance in some of the shows, the fans still loved him and flocked to all his performances.

Elvis's last appearance on stage, on June 26, 1977, in Indianapolis. He had missed several shows over the previous few months, amid increasing concerns over his health. After the show he returned home to Graceland to rest and recuperate over the summer, before the start of the next tour. The next tour never happened—in fewer than two months he was dead.

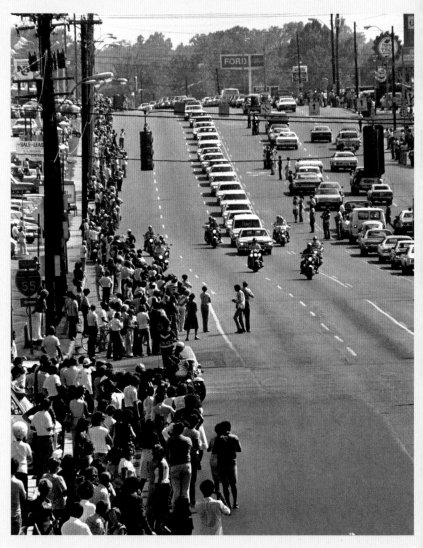

CHAPTER SIX

Only Believe

Right from the start, confusion surrounded the cause of Elvis's death, since the Shelby County Medical Examiner announced to the press that it was due to heart problems (cardiac arrhythmia, or irregular heartbeat) before the autopsy had been completed. In fact, the lab results later confirmed that his death was due to polypharmacy; traces of a total of 14 different medications were found in Elvis's system, with codeine at ten times the recommended level. Elvis had apparently taken the drug after the dental work carried out the day before his death—despite having a mild but long-standing allergy to it. No official announcement was made about the lab results, although rumors of drug abuse quickly began to circulate in the media. In 1979, Dr. Nichopoulos was charged with over-prescribing drugs to Elvis and briefly lost his medical license, but was later found not guilty of any criminal intent.

Elvis's funeral was a private service held at Graceland, with only 200 invited guests, although thousands of fans gathered outside. A cortege of 49 cars followed the white hearse that carried his body to Forest Hill Cemetery, where he was buried next to his mother. The following day an estimated 50,000 fans visited his tomb, and Vernon requested that each should be given a flower from the wreaths and arrangements that were banked up round the cemetery. It had taken 100 vans nearly four hours to move all the floral tributes from Graceland the day before, yet within a few hours they were all gone.

Just 11 days after the burial, three men made what was thought to be a bungled attempt to steal Elvis's body. Charges were dropped after the court was convinced that they had merely been trying to prove that the coffin was empty and that Elvis was still alive. There were fears that it might happen again, so just a couple of months later, both Elvis and his mother were removed from Forest Hill Cemetery and re-interred in the Meditation Garden at Graceland. The Meditation Garden also held a memorial plaque for Elvis's stillborn twin brother, Jesse Garon Presley, and Vernon was buried there after his death in 1979.

The entire Presley estate had been left to Lisa Marie in trust until she was 25, but Priscilla and the other trustees were alarmed to discover how little money was left. The Colonel had wasted no time in arranging a new marketing deal with Vernon, which meant that, for the next few years, he was earning far more from Elvis's name than the estate was. After Vernon's death in 1979, the executors of the Presley estate started an investigation and the courts later ruled that the contract Vernon had signed was void, so the Colonel had to give up all marketing rights.

In 1982 Graceland was opened to the public to raise money to protect Lisa Marie's inheritance, and the Presley

Opposite: Elvis's funeral cortege was led by a silver Cadillac and a police motorcycle escort, followed by a white hearse and seventeen white limousines.

estate also began to receive all the income generated through the use of Elvis's name. According to an estimate in *Life* magazine in 1984, the "Elvis industry" earned ten times more money in the seven years following his death than Elvis had earned in his 23 years of performing. When Lisa Marie turned 25 in 1993, the estate was worth an estimated $100 million and she elected not to take over, but to leave the existing management in place. Elvis Presley Enterprises, Inc. is now run as a business, controlling the rights to Elvis's name, and Graceland is a major tourist attraction, one of the most visited historic homes in America.

Elvis is perhaps even more famous today than when he was alive. In the weeks after his funeral, radio stations around the world started to play his music again and several of his records re-entered the charts. Although his music had changed almost out of recognition in the last few years of his life, his death focused attention on the early songs, when he had been a true artist and a major influence on the development of modern music. He was posthumously inducted into the Rock and Roll, Country, and Gospel Halls of Fame—the first artist to make it into all three.

Over the years there has been a constant stream of Elvis documentaries, films, and TV series, either telling his life story, looking at the making of a particular record or discussing his death. Many people who were close to Elvis have been persuaded to write about their memories of him, and countless books and articles have been published over the years, some flattering, some condemning. In 1988, rumors spread that he had faked his own death, after a book claiming he was still alive was published, along with a tape of him apparently talking about events that had happened after 1977. The tape was later discredited, but the rumors escalated and sightings of Elvis were reported all over the place. The stories became increasingly bizarre, placing him in unlikely locations around the world, and even on the moon. A few of the more obsessive fans seized on his connection with the BNDD and insisted that he had actually gone undercover as a narcotics investigator, or that he had merely become tired of his public lifestyle and had vanished to find a quieter life elsewhere.

However, most fans are content to remember their hero by visiting places of importance to him and collecting memorabilia. In 1992, the US Postal Service was persuaded to issue an Elvis stamp. Two designs were produced—one showing Elvis as a young rocker and the other the more mature, Vegas-style Elvis. Fans were asked to vote on which one they preferred. The young rocker won hands down, and 500 million stamps were printed—more than any other similar stamp.

Every year there is a Tribute Week in Memphis around the anniversary of Elvis's death, with dozens of Elvis-related events. People flock from across the globe to take part. At regular conventions around the world, thousands of fans still gather to listen to speeches, talk about Elvis and buy Elvis products. And then there are the Elvis impersonators; although they also existed before his death, there are now thousands of them around the world, some full-time, some part-time—including several black and Asian people, women and children. Most seem to choose to portray the 1970s Las Vegas Elvis, perhaps because that look is so instantly recognizable, and they often take their role extremely seriously, buying exact replicas of his outfits and closely copying his movements and style of delivery. A few have even had plastic surgery to make them look as much like the real Elvis as possible. And some, as well as performing as Elvis, keep up the act in their everyday lives.

There can be few entertainers in the history of the world who have inspired such devotion. Years after his death, stores are still full of his records, and his image is instantly recognizable in almost every country of the world. He has become much more than just a singer who died—he is now a true American folk hero.

Elvis himself once said, "When I was a boy, I was the hero in comic books and movies. I grew up believing in a dream. Now, I've lived it out. That's all a man can ask for."

Opposite: Elvis's flower-covered casket is carried into the mausoleum at Forest Hill Cemetery. The pall-bearers included Memphis Mafia members Joe Esposito, Charlie Hodge, and Lamar Fike, Dr. Nichopoulos, and Elvis's cousin Billy Smith.

Elvis has left the building…

Above: The hearse with its copper casket leaves Graceland, past saluting policemen. The funeral service had been held in the living room, with a sermon by Reverend Bradley of the Wooddale Church of Christ.

Left: Local florists were flooded with over 3,000 orders for flowers and they covered the lawn in front of Graceland. It took four hours to move the flowers to the cemetery before the funeral.

Fans gather

Above and right: The fans started to gather at the gates of Graceland as soon as Elvis's death was announced. By the day of the funeral, both sides of the road along the entire route from Graceland to the cemetery were lined with fans—an estimated crowd of 15–20,000.

Finally at rest

Opposite: After an apparent attempt was made to steal Elvis's body just after the funeral, he and his mother were both moved from Forest Hill and reburied in the Meditation Garden at Graceland, in October 1977. The gray stone mausoleum was surrounded by a bank of flowers and was just a few hundred feet away from Gladys Presley's grave in the same cemetery.

Left and below right: Even now, fans still come to Graceland on the anniversary of Elvis's death to pay their respects and leave floral tributes to their idol. On the evening of August 15, there is a candlelight procession at Graceland, which often takes many hours to file past his grave. It is the culmination of the Tribute Week that is held in Memphis every year.

Below left: The original memorial from Gladys Presley's grave in Forest Hill Cemetery, with the Italian statue specially commissioned by Elvis and Vernon just after her death.

Overleaf: The floral tributes from fans are often extremely elaborate and some are hand-crafted.

Overleaf inset: Elvis Presley's star on the Walk of Fame in Hollywood.

TO ELVIS IN MEMORIAM

ELVIS AARON PRESLEY

JANUARY 8, 1935
AUGUST 16, 1977

SON OF
VERNON ELVIS PRESLEY
AND
GLADYS LOVE PRESLEY
FATHER OF
LISA MARIE PRESLEY

HE WAS A PRECIOUS GIFT FROM GOD
WE CHERISHED AND LOVED DEARLY.

HE HAD A GOD-GIVEN TALENT THAT HE SHARED
WITH THE WORLD. AND WITHOUT A DOUBT,
HE BECAME MOST WIDELY ACCLAIMED,
CAPTURING THE HEARTS OF YOUNG AND OLD ALIKE.

HE WAS ADMIRED NOT ONLY AS AN ENTERTAINER,
BUT AS THE GREAT HUMANITARIAN THAT HE WAS,
FOR HIS GENEROSITY, AND HIS KIND FEELINGS
FOR HIS FELLOW MAN.

HE REVOLUTIONIZED THE FIELD OF MUSIC AND
RECEIVED ITS HIGHEST AWARDS.

HE BECAME A LIVING LEGEND IN HIS OWN TIME,
EARNING THE RESPECT AND LOVE OF MILLIONS.

GOD SAW THAT HE NEEDED SOME REST AND
CALLED HIM HOME TO BE WITH HIM.

WE MISS YOU, SON AND DADDY. I THANK GOD
THAT HE GAVE US YOU AS OUR SON.

Elvis's homes

Opposite above: Elvis's childhood home in Tupelo is now a tourist attraction—although it is furnished with home comforts the Presleys could never have afforded when they lived there.

Opposite below: The living room at Graceland has been kept very much as Elvis left it and the decor and furnishings are flamboyant. The stained glass peacock was specially designed for the room—although displaying peacock feathers indoors is supposed to bring bad luck.

Above: The 1928 Kimball grand piano that Priscilla gave Elvis as an anniversary present, and which she had covered in 24-carat gold leaf both inside and out. It was first placed in the music room at Graceland but is now displayed at Nashville's Country Music Hall of Fame.

Chronology

1933

17 Jun Gladys Love Smith and Vernon Elvis Presley are married

1935

8 Jan Elvis Aaron Presley is born at his parents' home, 306 Old Saltillo Road; his twin brother, Jesse Garon Presley, is stillborn

1937

10 Nov Vernon Presley is found guilty of forging a check

1938

25 May Vernon Presley is sentenced to serve three years at Parchman penal plantation, a Mississippi state penitentiary, and Gladys and Elvis are left to live on welfare

1940

10 Oct Vernon is released from prison early because of good behavior

1945

8 Jan Elvis receives his first guitar for his tenth birthday

3 Oct At the annual Mississippi–Alabama Fair and Dairy Show, held in Tupelo, Mississippi, Elvis sings "Old Shep" in a live competition and wins second-place prize of $5 and free admission to the fairground rides

1948

Aug Governor Jimmie "Pappy" Davis of Louisiana bestows the honorary title of "Colonel" on his friend Tom Parker

12 Sept The Presleys move overnight to Memphis, after Vernon is caught trucking for a bootlegger and is fired from his job

1949

20 Sept The Presleys move into federal-funded accommodation in Memphis and life becomes more stable for nearly three years

1951

3 Jun Elvis starts work at Precision Tools

1 Jul Elvis is fired when it is learned that he is under-age

1952

Mar Elvis plays at the Palm Club on Summer Avenue, Memphis, but the gig goes unnoticed

24 Dec Elvis sings "Old Shep" and "Cold, Cold Icy Fingers" at his school's Christmas concert to rave reviews

1953

8 Jan Vernon and Gladys pay $50 for a 1942 Lincoln Zephyr coupé, as an 18th-birthday present for Elvis

9 Apr At the "Annual Minstrel" at his school, Elvis sings a blues version of "Keep Them Icy Fingers Off Of Me." He receives an encore and sings a second song, which was either "'Til I Waltz Again With You" or "Old Shep"

26 May After hitchhiking to Meridian, Mississippi, Elvis sings at the First Jimmie Rodgers Memorial Talent Show at the Lamar Hotel and wins the second-place guitar prize with a country version of "I'm Left, You're Right, She's Gone" and a rock version of "Baby, Let's Play House"

3 Jun Elvis graduates from Class 202 at Humes High School

Summer Elvis records "My Happiness" and "That's When Your Heartache Begins" at Sam Phillips's Memphis Recording Service; he takes the original pressing and no copies are made

1954

4 Jan Elvis records "I'll Never Stand In Your Way" and "Casual Love Affair" at Sam Phillips's Memphis Recording Service; again, he takes the original pressing and no copies are made

Jan Dixie Locke becomes Elvis's first serious girlfriend

May Sam Phillips asks Elvis to sing "Without You," but is not impressed; however, he calls guitarist Scotty Moore and bass player Bill Black, and asks them to work with Elvis; the three rehearse for weeks at Phillips's Sun Studios

Jul Elvis gives his first interview, to editor Paul Ackerman of *Billboard*

Jul At the Bon Air Club, Memphis, Elvis sings "That's All Right, Mama" and "Blue Moon Of Kentucky," backed by Doug Poindexter and the Starlight Wranglers with Scotty Moore and Bill Black

5–6 Jul Elvis, Scotty Moore, and Bill Black record "That's All Right, Mama" and "Blue Moon of Kentucky" at Sun Studios

7 Jul Sam Phillips sends out DJ demos of the first record, and Dewey Phillips plays "That's All Right, Mama" on WHBQ 14 times in a row; later that evening, Elvis is interviewed on-air

11 Jul Elvis, Scotty Moore, and Bill Black, along with Johnny Bernero, record "Mystery Train" at Sun Studios

12 Jul Elvis and his parents sign a one-year contract with Scotty Moore

19 Jul Official release of the first record "That's All Right, Mama"/"Blue Moon of Kentucky", which quickly sells 20,000 copies

28 Jul The first published interview with Elvis appears in "The Front Row" in the *Press-Scimitar*

30 Jul Elvis appears in his first major concert, at the Overton Park Shell

7 Aug *Billboard* reviews "That's All Right, Mama," giving it a good write-up

Aug–Oct Elvis and the Blue Moon Boys perform several times in Texas and at the Eagle's Nest, Memphis whenever they can

9 Sept Marion Keisker of Sun Studios organizes a Memphis fanclub for Elvis and the Blue Moon Boys

25 Sept Elvis and the Blue Moon Boys appear at Nashville's Grand Ole Opry, but do not go down well; Elvis never performed there again

25 Sept Release of "Good Rockin' Tonight"/"I Don't Care If The Sun Don't Shine"

Oct Promoter Oscar "The Baron" Davis brings Elvis to the attention of his boss, Colonel Tom Parker; the Colonel comes to see him perform and they meet for the first time, at Taylor's restaurant, along with Scotty, Bill Black, the Baron, and Bob Neal

16 Oct Elvis and the Blue Moon Boys appear on a radio show, the *Louisiana Hayride*, which went out across the southern US on KWKH from Shreveport's Municipal Auditorium; he is an instant success

23 Oct Elvis and the Blue Moon Boys perform again on the *Louisiana Hayride*

Nov The DJs at *Billboard* put Elvis eighth on a list of most promising new hillbilly or country and western singers of 1954

6 Nov Elvis and the Blue Moon Boys perform on the *Louisiana Hayride* and afterward sign a one-year contract to appear every Saturday night

Nov The band goes on a concert tour through Texas, appearing at Boston, Lufkin, Longview, Odessa, and the Memphis Airport Inn

Dec Elvis and the Blue Moon Boys appear each week on the *Louisiana Hayride* show

10 Dec Elvis records "Milkcow Blues Boogie" at Sun Records

18 Dec "I'm Left, You're Right, She's Gone" and a version of "My Baby's Gone" are recorded at Sun Studios

1955

1 Jan The OK Group of New Orleans, Louisiana, hires Elvis for one-night performances on the radio at $300 a time

8 Jan "Milkcow Blues Boogie"/"You're A Heartbreaker" is released, but does not chart

Jan Colonel Parker sends Jimmy Rodgers Snow, Hank Williams' son, to see Elvis perform; he reports back that Elvis is provocative, sexy, and appeals to all women

Jan Elvis and the band appear at a series of concerts in Mississippi, Arkansas, Alabama, and Missouri

16 Jan Elvis and the band appear at a concert in Booneville, Mississippi, part of which is broadcast by WBIP. Further concerts follow at Eagle's Nest, Houston and Lake Pontchartrain, New Orleans

Feb Colonel Parker attempts to get RCA interested in Elvis, but although Steve Sholes, RCA's man in Nashville, is interested the record company is not

Feb Elvis and the band continue to appear on the *Louisiana Hayride* on Saturday nights and also play concerts in Carlsbad, New Mexico, Albuquerque, Texas, Louisiana, Arkansas, and Cleveland

Mar The band flies to New York City to audition for Arthur Godfrey's Talent Scouts, but is turned down

5 Mar Elvis makes his TV debut when the *Louisiana Hayride* is broadcast regionally from Shreveport, Louisiana

Mar Elvis and the boys appear in concerts in Tennessee, Louisiana, Arkansas, Mississippi, and Missouri

19 Mar Elvis appears live on the *Grand Prize Saturday Night Jamboree*, broadcast from Eagle's Hall in Houston, Texas, by KPRC-TV; he also records "I Got A Woman" at the same venue

28 Mar Part of a performance at the Circle Theater in Cleveland is broadcast on WERE radio

1 Apr "Baby, Let's Play House"/"I'm Left, You're Right, She's Gone" is released; the A-side causes a stir as it appears to hint at pre-marital sex

16 Apr Elvis performs for KRLD radio in Dallas, Texas

1 May Elvis performs in New Orleans and then begins a three-week tour through Chattanooga with Hank Snow's All-Star Jamboree

13 May Screaming teenage girls mob Elvis wherever he appears, and a concert in Jacksonville, Florida, causes a riot, with girls jumping on to the stage and trying to tear off his clothes, knocking police guards to the ground and trying to enter Elvis's dressing room

25 May Elvis performs at the Jimmie Rodgers Memorial Day Celebration in Meridian, Mississippi

31 May An afternoon concert in Midland, Texas is followed by a live radio appearance on *The Roy Orbison Show* in Odessa

26 Jun After a concert in Biloxi, Mississippi, Elvis meets June Juanico, whom he dates on and off for a year

Jul "Baby, Let's Play House" makes it into the *Billboard* Top Ten

25 Jul A famous picture of Elvis in a gold lamé tuxedo is taken by William S. Randolph at a concert in the 116th Field Artillery Armory in Tampa, Florida

6 Aug Release of "I Forgot To Remember To Forget"/"Mystery Train," which later goes into the *Billboard* country chart for 40 weeks

15 Aug Elvis signs a contract giving Colonel Parker the right to manage his career, although he is still bound to Bob Neal for another year

"Mystery Train" enters the *Billboard* country chart, staying there for 30 weeks

8 Sept Without Colonel Parker's knowledge, Elvis signs a new contract with the *Louisiana Hayride* for a further year from November 8; his payment increases from $18 a night to $200

Oct Atlantic Records bids $25,000 for Elvis to sign with them, but is turned down

10 Nov At the annual DJ convention in Nashville, Elvis secures the recording rights to "Heartbreak Hotel" from Mae Axton

13 Nov The Country & Western Disk Jockey Association names Elvis Most Promising Country Artist

19 Nov Colonel Parker, Elvis and Red West fly to New York City to meet Jean and Julian Aberbach of Hill & Range Music

20 Nov Sun Records' contract with Elvis is bought for $25,000 by RCA Victor, while Hill & Range Music buys Sam Phillips's Hi-Lo music publishing company for $15,000

Nov Elvis and Dixie Locke break up, as his new life keeps them apart too much

22 Nov Elvis signs a contract making Colonel Parker his exclusive representative

1956

5 Jan Colonel Parker does a deal with Hill & Range Music, establishing a 50/50 partnership for five years with the newly created Presley Music Inc to publish the songs Elvis records

9 Jan Elvis rehearses "Heartbreak Hotel," before recording it for RCA the following day along with "I Got A Woman;" the next day, he records "I Was The One" and "I'm Counting On You"

15 Jan RCA gives Elvis a new convertible

17 Jan Release of "Heartbreak Hotel"/"I Was The One"

28 Jan Elvis appears on Milton Berle's *Stage Show* on CBS TV. This was the first of several TV appearances including the Dorsey Brothers' *Stage Show* and Ella Fitzgerald's *Stage Show*.

30–31 Jan "Blue Suede Shoes" is recorded during a two-day studio session

15 Feb "I Forgot To Remember To Forget"/"Mystery Train" both reach No. 1 on the *Billboard* country chart, the first Elvis records to do so

22 Feb "Heartbreak Hotel" enters the *Billboard* Top 100 at No. 68 and the Country's Best Sellers in Stores chart at No. 9

29 Feb "I Was The One" enters the *Billboard* Top 100 at No. 84

1 Mar RCA is overwhelmed with 362,000 advance orders for the first LP, *Elvis Presley*

3 Mar RCA's Top 25 Best Sellers list contains six records by Elvis

7 Mar "Heartbreak Hotel" is No. 1 on the *Billboard* Country Best Sellers in Stores chart

13 Mar Release of the LP, *Elvis Presley*, which goes on to become the first in history to sell a million copies and stays in the *Billboard* extended-play album chart for a total of 68 weeks

15 Mar Colonel Parker becomes the sole official manager of Elvis

17 Mar Elvis appears on the St Patrick's Day *Stage Show* on CBS TV

28 Mar "Blue Suede Shoes" enters the *Billboard* Top 100 chart at No. 88

1 Apr Elvis does a screen-test in Los Angeles for Hal Wallis of Paramount Pictures

Apr "Heartbreak Hotel" is No. 1 on the *Billboard* pop chart and stays there for seven weeks; at the same time it is No. 1 on the country and western chart and No. 5 on the R&B chart

6 Apr Paramount Pictures signs Elvis to a seven-year, three-movie contract

May Release of "I Want You, I Need You, I Love You," which stays in the *Billboard* Top 100 for 24 weeks and reaches No. 3, also getting to No. 10 on the R&B chart and No. 1 for one week on the country chart; the flipside was "My Baby Left Me"

11 Apr *Variety* claims that "Heartbreak Hotel" has become the first Presley record to sell a million copies

23 Apr Elvis begins a four-week engagement at the New Frontier Hotel, Las Vegas, but the audience does not respond well to him and he only stays for two weeks

Apr Elvis has talks with Liberace, who becomes a major influence on how he dresses and presents himself

Jun RCA releases the EP "Elvis Presley," which goes on to stay in the *Billboard* Top 100 for 12 weeks, reaching No. 24

Jun *Time* nicknames Elvis "The Pelvis"

1 Jul Elvis appears on *The Steve Allen Show*, singing "Hound Dog" to a basset hound

20 Aug Elvis begins filming *Love Me Tender* in Hollywood for Twentieth Century Fox

3 Sept Although she does not drive, Elvis buys his mother Gladys a pink Cadillac

5 Sept "Don't Be Cruel"/"Hound Dog" reaches No. 1 on the *Billboard* Top 100

9 Sept *The Ed Sullivan* Show gets the highest ratings in television history when Elvis appears

19 Sept "Blue Moon" enters the *Billboard* Top 100 at No. 87

Sept In an interview in the *New York Daily News*, Elvis says there should be no draft, which encourages some young men to burn their draft cards

Sept Release of "Tryin' To Get To You"/"I Love You Because," "Blue Suede Shoes"/"Tutti Frutti" and "One-Sided Love Affair"/"Money Honey," none of which chart

25 Sept Rumors circulate that Elvis is romancing actress Debra Paget, and that they will marry

26 Sept Tupelo inaugurates Elvis Presley Day

30 Sept Cardinal Spellman speaks out against Elvis, and Gladys is distraught to hear her son condemned

Oct *Variety* names Elvis "King of Rock 'n' Roll" and he also appears on the cover of *Rock and Roll* magazine

Oct Elvis receives his draft questionnaire

3 Oct "I Don't Care If The Sun Don't Shine" enters the *Billboard* Top 100 at No. 77

8 Oct *Time* reveals that RCA has advance orders of one million for the single "Love Me Tender"—an all-time high

10 Oct "Love Me Tender"/"Any Way You Want Me" enters the *Billboard* Top 100 at No. 9

18 Oct Elvis gets into a fight with a gas station owner, who asks him to leave the gas station after his Cadillac draws a crowd of fans nearly causing a riot

19 Oct The LP *Elvis* is released

24 Oct Elvis earns a gold record for "Love Me Tender," his fifth of the year

27 Oct The front page of *Billboard* announces that the Army plans to give Elvis a GI haircut, which causes fans to panic

31 Oct Elvis starts to date Barbara Hearn

Nov The EPs "Elvis Vol 1" and "Elvis Vol 2" are released

7 Nov "Love Me" enters the *Billboard* Top 100 at No. 84, the LP *Elvis* enters the Best Selling Packaged Records—Popular Albums at No. 7 and "Love Me Tender" reaches No. 1 on the Top 100

14 Nov At a Liberace concert in the Riviera Hotel, Las Vegas, Elvis is in the audience and after the show the two of them exchange jackets

15 Nov The movie *Love Me Tender* opens in 500 theaters across the States and is a smash hit

21 Nov Colonel Parker owns Elvis completely, after he gets Bob Neal to sign a contract to that effect, and pays off Hank Snow in lieu of a finder's fee

23 Nov Louis Balint, an unemployed steelworker, is fined $19.60 for attacking Elvis because his wife's passion for the singer had broken up their marriage

28 Nov The movie *Love Me Tender* enters Variety's National Box Office Survey at No. 2

Dec Release of the EP "Love Me Tender"

15 Dec Elvis appears on the *Louisiana Hayride* for the last time

Dec "Heartbreak Hotel" is the *Billboard* No. 1 single for 1956

1957

4 Jan Accompanied by Las Vegas dancer Dorothy Harmony, Elvis has his pre-induction Army physical at Kennedy Veterans Hospital

6 Jan Elvis appears for the final time on *The Ed Sullivan Show*

Jan The Army announces that Elvis is classed 1-A for draft

21 Jan Start of the filming of *Loving You*, for Paramount

Jan   Release of "Too Much"/"Playing For Keeps," which stays in the *Billboard* Top 100 for 17 weeks, at No. 2 for four of them

5 Mar   Gladys and Vernon Presley see Graceland and persuade Elvis that he should buy it

7 Mar   Elvis pays $102,500 for Graceland, far outbidding an offer of $35,000 from the YMCA

Mar   RCA gives Elvis a suit made of gold lamé, from Nudie's Rodeo Tailors in Hollywood which he wears for the first time at a concert in Kiel Auditorium, St. Louis

10 Apr   "All Shook Up" reaches No. 1 on the *Billboard* Top 100 and stays there for eight weeks

13 May   Start of shooting on *Jailhouse Rock* for MGM, in Culver City

14 May   After swallowing the porcelain cap from one of his teeth, Elvis is rushed to the Cedars of Lebanon Hospital, California, with chest pains

June   "Teddy Bear"/"Loving You" is the first Elvis single to be distributed in the UK, and sells over a million copies

9 Jul   Premiere of *Loving You* at the Strand Theater in Memphis

27 Jul   "Teddy Bear"/"Loving You" hits No. 1 on the *Billboard* Top 100 and stays there for 17 weeks, it is also at No. 1 for one week on both the R&B and the country charts

30 Aug   According to a report in *The Spokane Review* the next day, Elvis whips 12,000 fans into a frenzy at a concert in the Memorial Stadium in Spokane, Washington; fans try to steal soil from the infield, because his feet have touched it

Sept   The single "Jailhouse Rock"/ "Treat Me Nice" is released in the UK and becomes the first Elvis record to enter the charts at No. 1 in England; it has already been released in the US and goes on to sell over three million copies in 12 months

Sept   Scotty Moore and Bill Black leave Elvis because of their poor pay and lack of credit, although they play at some further recording sessions

27 Sept   At Tupelo's Mississippi–Alabama Fair and Dairy Show, Elvis plays at a concert to benefit the Elvis Presley Youth Recreation Center, which he goes on to establish in his home town that December

28 Sept   The LP *Elvis Presley* reaches No. 1 on the *Billboard* extended-play album chart and stays there for six weeks

17 Oct   Premiere of *Jailhouse Rock* in Memphis

8 Nov   *Jailhouse Rock* opens across the country and goes on to make a profit within three weeks

19 Dec   Elvis receives his draft notice

1958

Jan   Release of "I Beg Of You," which stays in the *Billboard* Top 100 for 12 weeks, reaching No. 12, and getting to No. 4 on the R&B chart and No. 2 on the country chart

5 Mar   Filming starts on *King Creole* for Paramount and later moves to New Orleans

10 Mar   End of filming on *King Creole*

24 Mar   Elvis is inducted into the Army and is sent to Fort Chaffee, Arkansas

25 Mar   An Army haircut removes his famous ducktail hairstyle and sideburns

28 Mar   Elvis is sent to Fort Hood with his battalion for basic training

1 May   After the Colonel discovers that a soldier can live off-base if he has dependents in the area, Elvis moves his parents, along with his grandmother and Lamar Fike, into a rented house nearby and drives into the base every day for duty

June   Since her health has been failing for some time, Gladys returns to Memphis for treatment

1 Jul   *King Creole* is released to good reviews

5 Aug   Gladys is taken into hospital and Elvis is granted compassionate leave to visit her

11 Aug   Elvis receives his first RIAA Gold Disk Award for "Hard-Headed Woman"

14 Aug   Gladys dies of a heart attack in hospital

16 Aug   Gladys's funeral is held in Memphis and she is buried at Forest Hill Cemetery

24 Aug   As his unit is soon being sent to Germany, Elvis returns to basic training

19 Sept   With his Army unit, Elvis travels from Fort Hood to Brooklyn, New York

22 Sept   Elvis and his unit leave on the USS *General Randall* for Bremerhaven, Germany, where they disembark to transfer to Friedberg

10 Oct   The entourage moves into a rented house, and Elvis moves off base to join them

23 Oct   Bill Haley and the Comets play a concert in Frankfurt, which Elvis attends, posing afterwards in Haley's dressing room

Nov   Elvis goes on maneuvers along the Czech border

1 Nov   Elvis is dubbed "public enemy number one" by Russian leaders. Actress Venetia Stevenson flies to Germany to see Elvis

27 Nov   Elvis is promoted to Private First Class

20 Dec   After buying a used BMW 507 sports car from the company, Elvis agrees to pose for publicity shots

Dec   Elvis is named World's Outstanding Popular Singer, World's Outstanding Musical Personality and Favorite US Male Singer for 1958

1959

Jan   Robert Stephen Marquett, the son of an Army master sergeant, is pictured with Elvis and the photo becomes a 1959 March of Dimes poster

1 Jan   Vernon crashes his son's black Mercedes into a tree, and in the confusion the German newspapers report that Elvis has been killed; Vernon is unhurt, but his passenger, a young secretary, is paralysed for a short period

8 Jan   On his 24th birthday, Elvis is called by Dick Clark, who tells him he has been voted Best Singer of the Year, and that "King Creole" is Best Song of the Year; that evening, Dick Clark's *American Bandstand* program is dedicated to Elvis

3 Feb   Elvis is deeply upset by the death of Buddy Holly, Ritchie Valens, and Jiles Perry Richardson (the Big Bopper), along with their pilot, in a plane crash; all the musicians were friends

Apr   A war memorial is erected in Steinfurth by Elvis and his Army unit

May   In Friedberg, Elvis briefly dates Janie Wilbanks

1 Jun   Elvis is promoted to Specialist Fourth Class

3–9 Jun   Elvis gets tonsillitis and is sent to Frankfurt Military Hospital

21 Jun   Elvis and his entourage charter a plane and fly to Paris, where they stay at the Prince de Galles hotel on Avenue Georges V and frequent all the famous nightclubs

24–29 Oct   Elvis gets tonsillitis again and is sent to the General Hospital in Frankfurt

Nov   Priscilla Beaulieu is introduced to Elvis at a party

Nov   Vernon meets Dee Stanley, an American in Germany with her husband and family

Nov   After having karate lessons from Jurgen Seydel, Elvis has his photo taken in karate gi with a white belt

Dec   The magazine *Elvis Monthly* is published in the UK by Albert Hand

25 Dec   Elvis takes Priscilla to local festivities and meets her parents

1960

20 Jan   Elvis is promoted to Sergeant

Feb   The magazine *Elvis Monthly* is released in the US

17 Feb   The RIAA finally certifies the LP "Elvis" a Gold Disk—although it has already sold more than three million copies

Mar   A "Letter from Elvis" is printed in *Photoplay* and he appears in Army fatigues on the cover

Mar   *TV Radio Mirror* holds a contest to see who should be King of rock 'n' roll and Elvis is voted the winner

2 Mar   Elvis leaves Germany from Wiesbaden airport and arrives the following day at McGuire Air Force Base at Fort Dix

3 Mar   A photo of Elvis in uniform is featured on the front pages of newspapers across America; after being discharged, the ex-soldier tells the press there is no one special in his life and that he wants to concentrate on acting rather than singing. He then goes straight into the recording studio to produce some new songs

23 Mar   Traveling by train to Miami, the railway track is lined with fans and photographers trying to get a glimpse of Elvis

3 Apr   Release of the LP *Elvis Is Back*, which goes on to stay in the *Billboard* chart for 56 weeks, at No. 2 for three of them

3 Apr   "It's Now Or Never"/"A Mess Of Blues" is recorded, going on to enter the *Billboard* Hot 100 at No. 44 and climbing to No. 1 within five weeks; it

remains in the chart for 20 weeks, also reaching No. 7 on the R&B chart, and becomes the *Billboard* Vocal Single of 1960; it carries on selling through the years, achieving sales of well over 23 million copies

4 Apr   "Are You Lonesome Tonight" is recorded and makes the largest chart leap so far, entering the *Billboard* Hot 100 at No. 35 but jumping to No. 2 within seven days; it stays in the chart for 16 weeks, also reaching No. 22 on the country chart, No. 3 on the R&B chart and staying at No. 1 in the UK charts for four weeks

1 May   Elvis and his entourage arrive at the Beverly Wilshire to begin filming on *GI Blues* for Paramount

12 May   *The Frank Sinatra—Timex Special*, featuring Elvis and recorded at the Fontainebleau Hotel in Miami Beach, is broadcast on May 12 on ABCTV, and also includes a host of other stars including Nancy Sinatra, Sammy Davis Jr., and Peter Lawford

13 May   The change of style as featured on the Sinatra show upsets many fans; some critics accuse Elvis of deserting rock 'n' roll, or becoming lazy and no longer caring about the music, although others feel he has matured

Jun   *Movie Mirror* announces that "The King of Rock 'n' Roll is Dead!" and reports that Elvis is now conservative

Jun   During a trip to Las Vegas, Elvis's entourage is christened the "Memphis Mafia;" the name sticks

3 Jul   Vernon marries Dee Stanley, but Elvis refuses to attend the wedding

20 Jul   Vernon brings Dee and her three sons to Graceland, but they soon move out again to a house on Dolan Avenue

15 Aug   Filming begins on *Flaming Star* for Twentieth Century Fox

18 Aug   Preview of *GI Blues*, which becomes a big box-office draw despite being disliked by the critics

Sept The Mexican government bans all Elvis films after a showing of *GI Blues* in Mexico City causes a riot

4 Oct Filming finishes on *Flaming Star* and Elvis embarks on a short-lived affair with wardrobe assistant Nancy Sharp

30 Oct "It's Now Or Never"/"A Mess Of Blues" goes in at No. 1 in the UK charts, and stays there for eight weeks

11 Nov Filming begins on *Wild in the Country* for Twentieth Century Fox

23 Nov National release of *GI Blues*, which reaches No. 2 in *Variety's* list of top-grossing films

23 Nov A version of *Flaming Star* with only two songs is previewed in Westchester, California; it was later selected for general release and went into *Variety's* list of top-grossing films at No. 12. A version of the film with four songs is previewed, but is later dropped

Dec Elvis is inducted into the Los Angeles Indian Tribal Council by Chief Wah-Nee-Ota

1961

3 Jan Elvis returns to Los Angeles to finish filming on *Wild in the Country*

8 Jan On the set of *Wild in the Country*, Elvis celebrates his birthday with actress Hope Lange

18 Jan Filming finishes on *Wild in the Country*

8 Mar Governor Buford Ellington bestows the honorary title of "Colonel" on Elvis

14 Mar Elvis flies to California with his entourage to begin filming on *Blue Hawaii* for Paramount

24 Mar Elvis flies to Hawaii

25 Mar A benefit concert for the USS *Arizona* Memorial Fund, held at Bloch Arena in Pearl Harbor, Hawaii, raises $65,000

15 Jun *Wild in the Country* is premiered, then released nationwide

1 Jul The wedding of Red West and Patricia Boyd is attended by Elvis with Anita Wood

6–7 Jul Elvis and his entourage travel by bus from Nashville to Florida

11 Jul Filming begins on *Follow That Dream* for United Artists

Sept–Oct Elvis spends some time in Hollywood, briefly flying to Nashville to record more songs

5–14 Nov Elvis is coached for the boxing scenes in *Kid Galahad* by former junior welterweight champion Mushy Callahan

Nov Filming begins on *Kid Galahad* for United Artists

21 Nov *Blue Hawaii* is released nationally and, by the end of the year, has grossed $4.7 million

30 Nov Elvis is offered the lead in *Too Late Blues*, but the Colonel makes him turn it down

1962

8 Jan Dick Clark dedicates the broadcast of *American Bandstand* to Elvis on his birthday

Feb Colonel Parker persuades Elvis to turn down the part of Chance Wayne in *Sweet Bird of Youth*, the film of Tennessee William's play; the role goes to Paul Newman instead

7 Apr Elvis flies to Hawaii to begin filming on *Girls! Girls! Girls!* for Paramount

11 Apr Premiere of *Follow That Dream* in Ocala, Florida

15 May The cast return to Culver City to complete *Girls! Girls! Girls!*

23 May National release of *Follow That Dream*, which did not do well at the box office

June After protracted negotiations with her stepfather, Priscilla Beaulieu arrives in Los Angeles from Germany to spend some time with Elvis

27 Aug Filming begins on *It Happened at the World's Fair* for MGM

29 Aug National release of *Kid Galahad*, which goes on to gross $1.7 million by the end of the year

8 Sept Elvis arrives in Seattle for further filming on *It Happened at the World's Fair*, staying at the New Washington Hotel

Oct Release of "Return To Sender"/ "Where Do You Come From?," which reaches No. 2 on the *Billboard* Hot 100, No. 5 on the R&B chart and was No. 1 for three weeks in the UK

31 Oct Premiere of *Girls! Girls! Girls!* in Honolulu

Nov Elvis returns to Graceland for three weeks

21 Nov National release of *Girls! Girls! Girls!*, which goes on to gross $2.6 million by the end of the year

Dec Elvis is voted fifth top box-office draw by theater owners and receives three Norwegian Silver Record Awards for "Good Luck Charm"

Dec Priscilla's parents are persuaded to let her come to America to spend Christmas with Elvis at Graceland

1963

Jan Priscilla returns to Germany, but Elvis asks her stepfather if she can move to America and finish her education at a private school in Memphis

28 Jan Filming begins on *Fun in Acapulco* for Paramount; although some shots were done in Acapulco, Elvis only filmed in Hollywood on Paramount's lots

5 Mar Elvis is badly upset when his friend Patsy Cline, touring companion Lloyd "Cowboy" Copas, and Harold "Hawkshaw" Hawkins are killed in a plane crash

15 Mar Filming is completed on *Fun in Acapulco*

Mar Priscilla moves into Graceland with her parents' permission and is enrolled at the Immaculate Conception High School, an all-girl Catholic establishment

3 Apr Premiere of *It Happened at the World's Fair* in Los Angeles

10 Apr Nationwide opening of *It Happened at the World's Fair*, which went on to gross $2.25 million by the end of the year

29 May Priscilla graduates from the Immaculate Conception High School

15 Jul Filming begins on *Viva Las Vegas* for MGM; during the filming Elvis and his costar Ann-Margret have an affair

5 Oct Filming begins on *Kissin' Cousins* for MGM

21 Oct Filming finishes on *Kissin' Cousins*

27 Nov National release of *Fun in Acapulco*, which goes on to gross over $1.5 million by the end of the year

11 Dec *Love Me Tender* is shown on television

Dec Elvis is voted seventh top box-office draw by theater owners

1964

1 Jan Elvis is rejected in favor of George Hamilton to play Hank Williams in the film of his life, *Your Cheatin' Heart*, because Williams' widow feels the presence of Elvis would overshadow her husband's story

30 Jan The yacht *Potomac*, which had once been owned by President Franklin D. Roosevelt, is bought by Elvis

Feb *Movie Life* runs an article about Elvis marrying Ann-Margret, but it refers to their screen wedding in *Viva Las Vegas*

7 Feb The Beatles arrive in New York and Elvis sends them a congratulatory telegram

15 Feb Elvis donates the yacht *Potomac* to St. Jude's Children's Hospital

Feb–Mar *Kissin' Cousins* has sneak previews in North Long Beach, California and Phoenix, Arizona

9 Mar Filming begins on *Roustabout* for Paramount

11 Mar An award for Americanism is given to Elvis by Shelby County and Memphis business leaders

Apr *Kissin' Cousins* opens across the nation

Apr First publication of the newspaper *The Elvis Echo*, edited by Paulette Sansone

20 Apr Premiere of *Viva Las Vegas* in New York; filming finishes on *Roustabout*

30 Apr Elvis and Larry Geller meet for the first time when Geller comes to cut Elvis's hair; Geller persuades Elvis to study the occult

17 Jun National release of *Viva Las Vegas*, which goes on to gross over $4.5 million by the end of the year

22 Jun Filming begins on *Girl Happy* for MGM

Jul Elvis receives a South African Gold Record Award for "Kiss Me Quick" on the MGM lot of *Girl Happy*

1 Aug Johnny Burnette, a close friend of Elvis's, is drowned in California; Elvis is devastated

Aug The UK press report that Ann-Margret and Elvis plan to marry, although she denies saying anything

6 Oct Filming begins on *Tickle Me* for Allied Artists

11 Nov National release of *Roustabout*, which goes on to gross $3 million by the end of the year

Dec Elvis is voted sixth top box-office draw by theater owners and is presented with an award as Tennessee's Entertainer of the Year

1965

8 Jan Elvis celebrates his 30th birthday at Graceland

15 Mar Filming begins on *Harum Scarum* for MGM

Apr Elvis starts to visit the Self-Realization Fellowship Center and later meets its president, Sri Daya Mata

14 Apr National release of *Girl Happy*, which goes on to gross $3.1 million by the end of the year, despite poor reviews

25 May Filming begins on *Frankie and Johnny* for United Artists

28 May Premiere of *Tickle Me* in Atlanta, Georgia

7 Aug Filming begins on *Paradise, Hawaiian Style*

9–10 Aug Elvis is absent without explanation from the set of *Paradise, Hawaiian Style*

27 Aug The Beatles and Brian Epstein meet Elvis at his Bel Air home

21 Oct Bill Black, one of the Blue Moon Boys, dies during surgery for a brain tumor

24 Nov Premiere of *Harum Scarum* in Los Angeles

Dec Elvis moves from Perugia Way, Bel Air, to Rocca Place in Stone Canyon

1966

20 Feb Filming begins on *Spinout* for MGM

Feb President Lyndon Baines Johnson visits Elvis on the set of *Spinout*

Mar Felton Jarvis of RCA becomes producer of Elvis's recording sessions

31 Mar Premiere of *Frankie and Johnny* in Baton Rouge, Louisiana

6 Apr Filming finishes on *Spinout*

May A short promotional film for *Paradise, Hawaiian Style* is released

Jun Sneak previews of *Paradise, Hawaiian Style* in Memphis and New York City

11 Jun Filming begins on *Double Trouble* for MGM

6 Jul Nationwide release of *Paradise, Hawaiian Style*, which goes on to gross over $2.5 million by the end of the year

5 Sept Filming finishes on *Double Trouble*

7–13 Sept In an article, *Weekend* wonders if Elvis and Priscilla are secretly married

Sept Elvis rents an ultra-modern house in Palm Springs as a private retreat

12 Sept Filming begins on *Easy Come, Easy Go* for Paramount

13 Sept A sneak preview of *Spinout* is attended by members of the Presley family, but not Elvis, who is still filming *Easy Come, Easy Go*

28 Oct Filming finishes on *Easy Come, Easy Go*

1 Nov The RIAA certifies the LP *Elvis Presley* as a Platinum Disk after it has sold a million copies

23 Nov Nationwide release of *Spinout*

Dec Both her parents and the Colonel insist that it is time Elvis marries Priscilla or that she moves out of Graceland so, just before Christmas, he finally proposes

Dec Elvis is voted tenth top box-office draw by theater owners—it is the last time he appears in the poll

1967

9 Feb Elvis buys the Circle G Ranch in Walls, Mississippi

Mar Annette Day, co-star of *Double Trouble*, is given a white Mustang by Elvis

Mar Filming begins on *Clambake* for United Artists in Los Angeles

10 Mar After slipping in a bathroom, Elvis suffers mild concussion

22 Mar National opening of *Easy Come, Easy Go*, which goes on to gross over $1.95 million by the end of the year

5 Apr Nationwide release of *Double Trouble*, which soon grosses $1.6 million

1 May Elvis marries Priscilla Beaulieu at the Aladdin Hotel, Las Vegas, in a private ceremony

2–6 May Elvis and Priscilla honeymoon in Palm Springs, California, and then go on to the Circle G Ranch, accompanied by some of the Memphis Mafia

7 May Elvis and Priscilla move to a new home in Hillcrest Road, Beverly Hills

29 May A second wedding ceremony is held at Graceland, as many people were excluded from the first

Jun *TV and Movie Guide* speculates that Nancy Sinatra might steal Elvis from Priscilla

12 Jun Filming begins on *Speedway* for MGM, which also stars Nancy Sinatra

Jun An article in *Screen Stories* suggests that Nancy Sinatra and Elvis are romantically involved

8 Sept Filming finishes on *Speedway*

9 Sept Elvis flies to Nashville, leaving Priscilla in Bel Air

18 Oct Filming begins on *Stay Away, Joe* for MGM in Arizona

Nov The cover of *Screen Life* features Elvis, and reports that he is to be a father

22 Nov Release of *Clambake*, which gets mixed reviews

3 Dec A special radio show, *Season's Greetings From Elvis*, is aired on RCA

8 Dec TV premiere of *Tickle Me* on CBS TV's *Friday Night at the Movies*

Dec Elvis receives a Grammy Award for Best Sacred Performance for "How Great Thou Art;" a pop poll names him No. 1 Male Singer and No. 1 Music Personality in America

31 Dec The Manhattan Club in Memphis is hired by Elvis for a New Year's Eve party with 500 guests, but Elvis himself does not attend

1968

Jan Elvis announces that he wants to do a singing tour of Europe, but the plan does not come to anything

1 Feb Lisa Marie Presley is born at the Baptist Memorial Hospital

Feb Release of *Elvis: Gold Records, Vol 4*

7 Feb Nick Adams, a close friend of Elvis's, commits suicide and Elvis is deeply affected

8 Feb *Playboy* magazine honors Elvis in its feature on the year's music scene

5 Mar Elvis flies to California for a recording session

8 Mar National distribution of *Stay Away, Joe*

25 May At a karate tournament in Honolulu, Elvis meets martial arts expert Mike Stone and suggests he teaches Priscilla

May Priscilla buys a 1928 Kimball grand piano and has it gold-leafed inside and out; she gives it to Elvis on their first wedding anniversary

15 Jun Elvis and Priscilla fly to Honolulu to see the USS *Arizona* Memorial

Jun *TV Times* reports that Elvis fans no longer scream when he appears

27–30 Jun Elvis tapes a TV special for NBC TV, and is persuaded to appear in black leather and go back to his musical roots

Jul Filming begins on *Live a Little, Love a Little* for MGM in Los Angeles

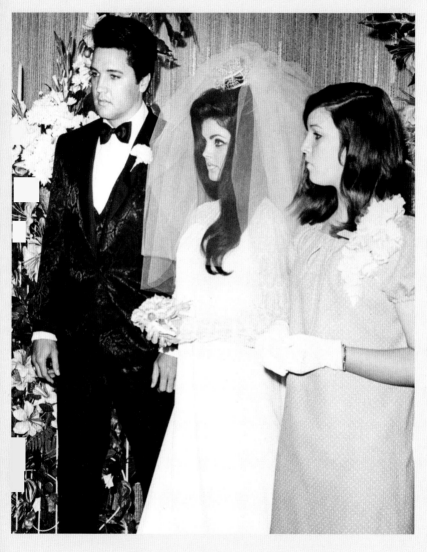

4 Jul   Elvis donates his Rolls-Royce Phantom V to a charity auction; it raises $35,000

22 Jul   Work commences on *Charro!* for National General in Arizona

30 Sept   The funeral of Dewey Phillips in Memphis, which Elvis attends

Oct   Priscilla and Elvis are featured on the cover of *Screen Life*, with an article about them wanting another baby

23 Oct   Release of *Live a Little, Love a Little*

28 Oct   Filming begins on *The Trouble with Girls* for MGM

3 Dec   The comeback TV special *Elvis* is broadcast on NBC TV and is the highest-rated program that week

4 Dec   The *New York Times* reports that Elvis has found his way home, and fans rush to buy his records again

31 Dec   *Elvis* is shown in the UK on BBC2

1969

10 Mar   Filming begins on *Change of Habit* for Universal and NBC in Los Angeles

13 Mar   National release of *Charro!*, which the fans love as Elvis looks handsome and rugged in a beard

Apr   Gospel singer Clara Ward and Blues singer Mahalia Jackson visit Elvis on the set of *Change of Habit*

2 May   Filming of *Change of Habit* is completed

May   Elvis decides that he no longer wants to act in movies, but would like to return to singing

21 May   The Circle G Ranch is sold and the horses moved to Graceland

1 Jun   Elvis goes on a diet to lose weight for his Las Vegas shows, before rehearsals begin in July

15 Jun   "In the Ghetto" is certified gold by the RIAA

31 Jul   At the International Hotel, Las Vegas, Elvis appears live in concert for the first time in eight years

1 Aug   Elvis tells reporters that he plans a world tour, but it does not come off

2 Aug   A gold belt is awarded to Elvis at the International Hotel for "the world's championship attendance record"

Aug   Fans travel from all over the world to see Elvis's Vegas shows

Aug   After a press conference, *Rolling Stone* reports that Elvis is "supernatural," *Variety* calls him a "superstar" and *Newsweek* compliments him on his staying power

Sept   "Suspicious Minds"/"You'll Think Of Me" is released and goes into the *Billboard* Top 100 for 15 weeks, reaching No. 1 in November for one week

22 Aug   The *Elvis* TV comeback special is broadcast again

3 Sept   National release of the film *The Trouble with Girls*

10 Nov   National release of the film *Change of Habit*

12 Dec   The LP *From Memphis to Vegas/From Vegas to Memphis* is certified gold by the RIAA

1970

21 Jan   "Don't Cry Daddy" sells a million copies and is certified gold by the RIAA

26 Jan   A new season of concerts begins at the International Hotel, Las Vegas

23 Feb   Elvis's 57th and last concert of the run at Las Vegas

27 Feb   The first concert of a three-day booking at Houston Astrodome, with Elvis performing two shows a night

1 Mar   Elvis flies back to Memphis to rest; after checking into the Baptist Memorial Hospital, he is informed that he has glaucoma in his left eye

1 Jun   Felton Jarvis leaves RCA to manage Elvis's recording career

10 Aug   The first concert in a new season at the International Hotel, Las Vegas

14 Aug   A paternity suit is filed against Elvis by Patricia Parker, a Hollywood waitress; her son Jason is born on October 19, 1970

26 Aug   Threats to kidnap or kill Elvis during a show are received; the FBI are called, but it turns out to be a hoax

7 Sept   The last concert of Elvis's current Las Vegas season

8 Sept   Nancy Sinatra opens at the International Hotel, Las Vegas; Elvis, Priscilla, Vernon, and Dee are in the audience; Priscilla returns home after the concert, but Elvis flies to Arizona

9 Sept   Elvis gives a concert at the Veterans Memorial Coliseum in Phoenix, Arizona, and goes on to appear in St. Louis, Detroit, Miami Beach, Tampa, and Mobile over the next few days

Oct   Elvis becomes a special deputy in Memphis so he can legally carry a gun

Oct   Elvis has 14-carat gold necklaces made for all the members of the Memphis Mafia, inscribed with "TCB" (standing for Taking Care of Business) and a lightning-bolt

Nov   Elvis tells the press that his marriage has difficulties

11 Nov   The premiere of *Elvis—That's The Way It Is*, a film of concerts and recording sessions, in Phoenix, Arizona; Portland, Oregon dubs this date Elvis Presley Day, when Elvis performs at the Memorial Coliseum. During the month Elvis also gave concerts at Englewood in New Jersey, Oakland, Seattle, San Francisco, Los Angeles, San Diego, Oklahoma City, and Denver

1 Dec   Elvis meets Vice President Agnew

3 Dec   Elvis spends $20,000 on guns in a three-day shopping spree

5 Dec Elvis attends George Klein's wedding in Las Vegas, for which he has paid

21 Dec During a meeting with President Nixon, Elvis is given a Narcotics Bureau badge since he has offered to work undercover to help stamp out drug abuse and subversive elements in America

28 Dec At Sonny West's and Judy Morgan's wedding in Memphis, Elvis is best man and Priscilla matron of honor

30 Dec Elvis is taken on a tour of FBI headquarters in Washington DC

1971

9 Jan Elvis is voted one of the Ten Outstanding Young Men of America by the Jaycees—members of the Junior Chamber of Commerce, a civic organization for business and community leaders; it is to be the only award Elvis collects in person

Jan–Feb A season of 57 concerts at the International Hotel, Las Vegas

27 Feb Elvis flies to Memphis for seven days, then drives on to Nashville for a recording session

4 May *Look* magazine features Elvis on its cover, with the first of a two-part account extracted from *Elvis: A Biography* by Jerry Hopkins

21 May "Suspicious Minds" is named the Most Outstanding Single to be recorded in Memphis

1 Jun The birthplace of Elvis in Tupelo is opened to the public

20 Jul Elvis plays the first of 28 concerts at the Sahara Tahoe Hotel in Stateline, Nevada followed by another season of 57 shows at the Hilton Hotel in Las Vegas

Aug Elvis and Priscilla move into a new house in Monovale, and Hillcrest is put up for sale

1 Sept Elvis buys his first Stutz Blackhawk coupe—he eventually owns three

8 Sept The Bing Crosby Award is given to Elvis by the National Academy of Recording Arts and Sciences

24 Oct A 12-hour radio show, *The Elvis Presley Story*, is produced by Jerry Hopkins and Ron Jacobs

Nov Elvis performs concerts in Minneapolis, Cleveland, Louisville, Philadelphia, Baltimore, Boston, Cincinnati, Houston, Dallas, Tuscaloosa, Kansas City, and Salt Lake City

Nov After Elvis passes a lie-detector test and a blood test, which prove he is not the father of Patricia Parker's son, she drops her paternity suit

30 Dec Elvis tells his companions that Priscilla has left him

31 Dec The *Elvis Presley Album* is issued by *Screen Star*, with Elvis featured on every page

1972

26 Jan The first of a new season of 57 concerts at the Las Vegas Hilton

Feb Priscilla tells Elvis that she has been having an affair with Mike Stone

Apr A series of concerts are played at Buffalo in New York, Detroit, Dayton, Knoxville, Hampton Roads in Virginia, Richmond, Roanoke, Indianapolis, Charlotte, Greensboro, Macon, Jacksonville, Little Rock, San Antonio, and Albuquerque; many of them are filmed for the documentary *Elvis on Tour*

6 Jun Elvis plays the opening concert of four at Madison Square Garden in New York followed by concerts in Fort Wayne and Evansville in Indiana, Milwaukee, Chicago, Forth Worth, Wichita, and Tulsa

6 Jul Elvis meets Linda Thompson, a former beauty queen

26 Jul Elvis and Priscilla are legally separated

4 Aug The opening concert of 63 at the Las Vegas Hilton

18 Aug Elvis files for divorce from Priscilla

4 Sept Elvis appears in the last in the series of Las Vegas concerts and, at a press conference, the Colonel confirms details of an NBC television special to be broadcast the following January

Sept Linda Thompson moves into Graceland

20 Oct Television premiere of *Change of Habit* on NBC's *Friday Night at the Movies*

1 Nov Release of *Elvis on Tour*, which grosses nearly half a million dollars in one week

Nov A series of concerts are played in Lubbock, Tucson, El Paso, Oakland, San Bernadino, Long Beach, and Honolulu

Dec A Grammy for Best Inspirational Performance is awarded for the LP *He Touched Me*; *Elvis on Tour* is voted Best Documentary of 1972 by the Hollywood Foreign Press Association and nominated for a Golden Globe Award

1973

9 Jan Elvis arrives in Honolulu to begin rehearsals for *Elvis: Aloha From Hawaii*

14 Jan *Elvis: Aloha From Hawaii* is broadcast to 40 countries worldwide

15 Jan A second broadcast of *Elvis: Aloha From Hawaii* is seen in 28 European countries

18 Jan Elvis and his entourage fly to Las Vegas and rehearsals begin for the opening of a season in Las Vegas

26 Jan Elvis performs the opening concert of 54 at the Las Vegas Hilton

Jan Elvis gives Muhammad Ali a flamboyant, jewel-encrusted robe with "People's Champion" inscribed across the back; Ali wears it before his February 14 fight against Joe Bugner in Las Vegas

Feb Due to the interaction of the cocktail of drugs he is now taking, Elvis misses several concerts in Las Vegas and is treated by a succession of doctors

18 Feb At Elvis's midnight show, four men rush on to the stage, apparently to attack Elvis, who knocks one back into the audience; the others are removed by security, but they turn out to be over-excited fans

23 Feb Elvis finishes the final concert in Las Vegas, but stays on to see Ann-Margret opening and several other shows

9 Mar Returning to Graceland, Elvis recuperates with Linda Thompson and the Memphis Mafia

2 Apr Elvis persuades Ed Parker to award him a sixth-degree black belt in kenpo karate

4 Apr *Elvis: Aloha From Hawaii* is expanded and broadcast as a TV special across the US on NBC TV

Apr Elvis persuades Kang Rhee to award him a seventh-degree black belt in *Pasaryu* karate

Apr Concerts are played in Phoenix, Anaheim, Fresno, San Diego, Portland, Spokane, Seattle, and Denver

4 May Elvis is due to play 25 concerts at the Sahara Tahoe Hotel in Stateline, Nevada, but several concerts are cancelled due to illness, as years of prescription drug abuse begin to take their toll

13 May After a special Mother's Day concert, Elvis donates money to the Barton Memorial Hospital in memory of his mother

18 May Ill and exhausted, Elvis returns to Memphis

May A private investigator, John O'Grady, is hired to investigate where Elvis is getting his prescription drugs

Jun Concerts are played in Mobile, Atlanta, Uniondale, Nassau, Pittsburgh, Cincinnati, St. Louis, Nashville, and Oklahoma City. After returning to Memphis in July, Elvis begins a series of recording sessions

6 Aug The first concert in a planned series of 59 at the Las Vegas Hilton, although Elvis misses two due to illness

Aug After a major argument the partnership of Colonel Parker and Elvis breaks up, but is soon re-instated

9 Oct The divorce of Elvis and Priscilla is finalized in Santa Monica

Oct Elvis is hospitalized for two weeks after an extreme drug reaction and is put through a drug withdrawal program

Nov *Movie World* features Elvis and Priscilla on its cover and reports that Elvis has collapsed after the divorce

10–16 Dec Elvis records several songs in a session at Stax Studios in Memphis, but using a mobile recording unit provided by RCA

1974

Jan Colonel Parker and Elvis form Boxcar Enterprises to handle the merchandising of Elvis-related products not connected to movies or records; Boxcar Records is also created

26 Jan The first concert in a series of 29 at the Las Vegas Hilton ending February 9

Mar *Silver Screen* features Elvis on its cover and an article speculates that he will marry Linda Thompson

Mar Concerts are played in Tulsa, Houston, Monroe in Louisiana, Auburn in Alabama, Montgomery, Charlotte, Roanoke, Hampton Roads, Richmond, Greensboro, Murfreesboro in Tennessee, Knoxville, and Memphis

Mar Dr. George Nichopoulos (Dr. Nick) attends Elvis full time during the tour so he can monitor his drug intake

May Concerts are played in San Bernadino, Los Angeles, and Fresno

followed by 22 concerts at the Sahara Tahoe Hotel in Stateline, Nevada

Jun During a 21-day tour, concerts are played in Fort Worth, Baton Rouge, Amarillo, Des Moines, Cleveland, Providence, Philadelphia, Niagara Falls, Columbus, Louisville, Bloomington, Milwaukee, Kansas City, Omaha, and Salt Lake City

19 Aug The first concert in a planned series of 29 at the Las Vegas Hilton; Elvis is ill and has to cancel two performances

Aug Linda Thompson is replaced by Sheila Ryan as Elvis's official girlfriend

19 Sept Linda Thompson appears back on the scene

29 Sept Local papers are enthusiastic after Elvis performs at a concert at the Olympian Stadium in Detroit

Oct Concerts are played in St. Paul in Minnesota, Dayton, Indianapolis, Wichita, San Antonio and Abilene followed by eight concerts at the Sahara Tahoe Hotel in Stateline, Nevada

Nov *Rolling Stone* reports that Elvis is still a superstar and he wins a Grammy for Best Inspirational Performance for "How Great Thou Art," which is featured on the LP *Elvis Recorded Live*

Dec Elvis recuperates from a strenuous year at Graceland and an article in *Celebrity* comments on his poor health

1975

29 Jan Elvis is rushed to hospital at midnight with severe stomach pains, and is admitted to get his drug use back under control

5 Feb Elvis's father Vernon has a heart attack and is admitted to the same hospital

10–13 Mar Elvis records at RCA's Hollywood studios

18 Mar The first of a scheduled 29 shows at the Las Vegas Hilton

28 Mar   Barbra Streisand talks to Elvis about taking the costarring role in the remake of *A Star is Born*, but the Colonel handles negotiations and the project founders

Apr   Elvis buys a 96-passenger Convair 880 plane, which he redecorates in blue and white, and christens the *Lisa Marie*. It is delivered on November 10

Apr–Jul   Concerts are played in Macon, Jacksonville, Tampa, Lakeland, Murfreesboro, Atlanta, Monroe, Lake Charles in Louisiana, Huntsville in Alabama, Mobile, Houston, Dallas, Shreveport, Jackson, Memphis, Oklahoma City, Terre Haute in Indiana, Cleveland, Charleston, Niagara Falls, Springfield, New Haven, Uniondale, Norfolk, and Greensboro

5 May   Elvis plays a benefit concert at the State Fair Coliseum in Jackson, Mississippi, and raises $108,000 for hurricane survivors in McComb, Mississippi

Jul   Elvis has cosmetic surgery to give his eyes a more youthful look

23–24 Jul   During a show at Asheville, North Carolina, Elvis gives away a $6,500 ring to a fan in the audience

27 Jul   After buying 14 Cadillac Eldorados, Elvis gives them all away

Aug   Priscilla and Mike Stone split up; Priscilla begins her acting career; Elvis is still in poor health and is putting on weight

18 Aug   Although he is due to perform a series of concerts at the Las Vegas Hilton, most of them are canceled due to Elvis's poor health

21 Aug   Elvis is admitted to hospital for two weeks and attempts are made to sort out some of his medical problems

Aug   Linda Thompson leaves to pursue an acting career, and Elvis briefly begins seeing Jo Cathy Brownlee

10 Nov   The *Lisa Marie* is finally delivered

28 Nov   Elvis flies to Las Vegas to rehearse for 17 shows at the Las Vegas Hilton, and Linda Thompson returns briefly to support him

31 Dec   A New Year's Eve concert in Pontiac, Michigan, breaks concert receipt records

1976

Jan   Elvis buys five cars and gives them away

22 Jan   A new agreement giving the Colonel 50/50 partnership on live dates comes into effect

Feb   *Movie Stars* features Elvis and Linda Thompson, with an article speculating that they will marry—in fact they are already well on the way to splitting up

2–8 Feb   Elvis records at Graceland, using temporary equipment installed by RCA

20 Apr   Elvis invests in Presley Center Courts, Inc., which plans to run racquet-ball clubs; he is a 25 percent partner, along with his physician, Dr. George Nichopoulos, Joe Esposito, and real estate developer Michael McMahon; Elvis pulls out when the venture is proved to be losing money

Apr–Jun   Concerts are played in Kansas City, Omaha, Denver, San Diego, Long Beach, Seattle, 15 shows at the Sahara Tahoe Hotel in Stateline, Nevada, Bloomington, Ames in Iowa, Oklahoma City, Odessa in Texas, Lubbock, Tucson, El Paso, Fort Worth, Atlanta, Omaha, Buffalo, Rhode Island, Largo in Maryland, Philadelphia, Richmond, and Greensboro

13 Jul   Vernon fires Red and Sonny West, along with Dave Hebler

Jul–Aug   Concerts are performed at Shreveport, Baton Rouge, Fort Worth, Tulsa, Memphis, Louisville, Charleston, Syracuse, Rochester, Hartford, Springfield, New Haven, Hampton Roads, Roanoke, San Antonio, Houston, Mobile, Tuscaloosa, and Macon

Sept–Oct   Elvis performs concerts in Jacksonville, Florida, Alabama, Arkansas, Duluth, Minneapolis, Sioux Falls, Madison, South Bend, Kalamazoo, Champaign, Cleveland, Evansville, Fort Wayne, Dayton and Carbondale, Illinois

29 Oct   Another recording session is arranged at Graceland, but Elvis is not well enough to do much work

19 Nov   Elvis meets Ginger Alden, a former beauty queen

Nov   Billy Carter, the President's brother, comments that Elvis is guarded better than the president after he and his wife visit Graceland

Nov   Elvis performs a series of concerts in Nevada, Oregon, and California, and Ginger Alden is invited to join him; Linda Thompson finally leaves for good

2 Dec   A new season of 15 concerts begins at the Las Vegas Hilton; the last is on December 12 and this time Elvis does not miss any performances

Dec   Elvis gives Ginger a Lincoln Mark V

9 Dec   Vernon is admitted to hospital with a suspected heart attack

27 Dec   The first of five concerts is performed in Wichita, Kansas; the others are in Texas, Alabama, Georgia and Pennsylvania

1977

Jan   Priscilla and Elvis are featured on the cover of *TV Star Parade*, with an article speculating that they have secretly remarried

Jan   Elvis spends his birthday with Ginger and her sister Rosemary in Palm Springs

20 Jan   A recording session is scheduled in Nashville, but Elvis cancels due to a sore throat

26 Jan   Elvis proposes to Ginger and gives her a diamond ring

1 Feb   Elvis and Ginger celebrate Lisa Marie's 9th birthday with her in LA

Feb–Mar   A series of 17 concerts are played in Florida, Alabama, Georgia, South Carolina, Tennessee, North Carolina, Arizona, Texas, Oklahoma, and Louisiana

3 Mar   Elvis takes Ginger and her family on a two-week vacation to Hawaii

Apr   A series of concerts is booked through North Carolina, Michigan, Ohio, Wisconsin, Minnesota, and Illinois, but Elvis collapses during the tour, and is taken back to Memphis and admitted to the Baptist Memorial Hospital

5 Apr   Elvis leaves hospital and spends some time recuperating at Graceland

Apr   Elvis argues with Ginger and invites Alicia Kerwin to accompany him on a trip to Las Vegas and Palm Springs

May–Jun   A series of 23 concerts is performed across 18 states with only 16 days' rest during the punishing schedule; Ginger accompanies Elvis for most of the time

May   Newspapers report that the Colonel is planning to sell Elvis's contract to pay off his gambling debts

1 Jun   The Colonel announces details of a forthcoming CBS concert special, to be filmed on the next tour

18 Jun   *Photoplay* awards Elvis Gold Medal Awards for Favorite Variety Star and Favorite Rock Music Star

27 Jun   Elvis returns to Graceland to recuperate

Jul   Release of "Way Down"/"Pledging My Love," which goes into the *Billboard* country chart for 17 weeks, reaching No. 1 in August; it also spends 21 weeks in the Top 100 chart, reaching No. 18, and reaches No. 14 on the easy listening chart; in the UK it becomes Elvis's 17th No. 1 record

Jul   The book, *Elvis: What Happened?*, is published, written by Steve Dunleavy and based on material from the three ex-members of the

Memphis Mafia: Red West, Sonny West, and Dave Hebler

Jul–Aug   Lisa Marie arrives at Graceland for a two-week visit; Elvis rents the Libertyland amusement park for several hours after closing time as a present for Lisa Marie and her friends

16 Aug   Elvis is found dead in his bathroom at Graceland by Ginger Alden; the cause of death is announced as a heart attack, but the later autopsy rules that he died from a drug overdose

17 Aug   With his body lying in state at Graceland, thousands of fans congregate outside, waiting to file past the coffin and get one last glimpse of Elvis

18 Aug   Elvis's funeral is held at Graceland, and he is laid to rest next to his mother at Forest Hill Cemetery

23 Aug   The Colonel convinces Vernon to sign a contract giving all rights to the marketing of Elvis-related products to Boxcar Enterprises; 50 percent of income is to be distributed equally between the Colonel and the Elvis Presley estate, with the remaining 50 percent for expenses and salaries; anything left after expenses is to be divided 56 percent to the Colonel and the rest between the estate and Tom Diskin

21 Aug   RCA reports that it has sold over eight million Elvis records in the six days since his death

29 Aug   Three men attempt to steal Elvis's body; charges are later dropped when the court believes they were trying to prove the coffin was empty and that Elvis is still alive

7 Sept   A shorter version of the documentary *Elvis on Tour* is shown on NBC TV to top ratings

12 Sept   "Way Down" is certified gold by the RIAA

3 Oct   CBS TV shows *Elvis in Concert*, a one-hour special that was filmed during his last tour

27 Oct   The bodies of Elvis and his mother are removed from Forest Hill Cemetery and re-interred at Graceland in the Meditation Garden

Nov   Elvis's physician, Doctor Nichopoulos suspended while the court investigates his prescription of drugs to Elvis

Nov   A Broadway show, *Elvis Lives*, wins the *New York Evening Standard* award for Best Musical of the Year

20 Nov   A three-hour television special, *Memories of Elvis*, is broadcast on NBC TV

1978

Jan   Elvis has left his entire estate to Lisa Marie, but Priscilla and the other trustees are horrified to discover there is no money left

1 Feb   *Playboy* inducts Elvis into its Music Hall of Fame

16–18 Aug   On the first anniversary of Elvis's death, thousands of fans gather outside Graceland

1–10 Sept   An Elvis Presley Convention is held at the Las Vegas Hilton—it becomes an annual event

8 Sept   A bronze statue of Elvis is unveiled in the lobby of the Las Vegas Hilton

1979

Jan   Investigations into Elvis's finances reveal he was not a member of Broadcast Music Inc., and so has probably lost millions of dollars in royalty payments

8 Jan   The anniversary of Elvis's birth is celebrated in Memphis and Tupelo, and becomes an annual event

11 Feb   ABC TV broadcasts *Elvis*, the story of his life with Kurt Russell playing Elvis and Shelley Winters as Gladys

Apr   A newsletter about Elvis, called *Reflections*, is started by two ex-members of the Memphis Mafia

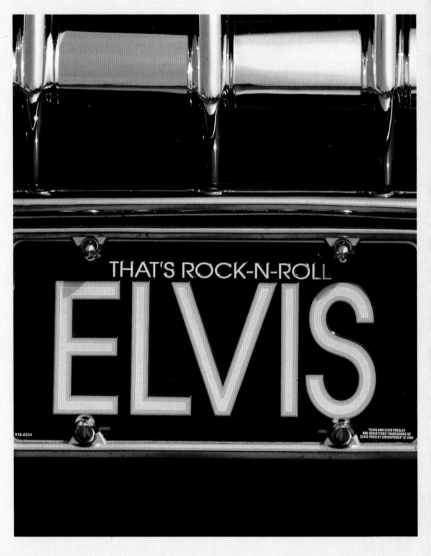

May Two tons of gray marble from Elvis's first tomb at the Forest Hill Cemetery are bought by Bill Carwile; he cuts it up into 44,000 small pieces, which he sells for $80 each

26 Jun Vernon dies of heart failure, and is later buried next to Elvis and Gladys

17 Aug An Elvis Presley Chapel is dedicated in Elvis Presley Park in Tupelo

1980

8 Feb NBC TV broadcasts *Elvis Remembered: Nashville to Hollywood*, which is a shortened version of *Nashville Remembers Elvis on His Birthday*

8 May Minnie Mae Presley, Elvis's grandmother, dies in Memphis

24 Jun Singer Margot Heine Kuzma alleges in the German *Globe* that her son Leroy is the son of Elvis

1981

The IRS claims that Elvis's estate owes $14.6 million in inheritance taxes, plus a further $2.3 million in tax interest; to raise funds and protect her daughter's inheritance, Priscilla plans to open Graceland to the public

3 Apr Premiere in Memphis of a documentary, *This is Elvis*, made by Warner Brothers

Jul The courts decide that Boxcar Enterprises has no right to distribute Elvis-related merchandise

Jul–Aug At the Las Vegas Hilton, *Elvis, An American Musical* is performed

1982

7 Jun The downstairs rooms at Graceland are opened to the public

Oct Release of *The Elvis Medley*, which goes on to stay in the *Billboard* Top LPs chart for nine weeks

1983

8 Jan An Elvis Presley Museum is opened in London

1984

Aug *Life* runs an article pointing out that the Elvis Presley industry is earning ten times as much as he did when he was alive

Aug–Nov The interior of Graceland is filmed for a video, *Elvis Presley's Graceland*; Elvis is posthumously awarded the WC Handy Award from the Blues Foundation for "keeping the blues alive;" Elvis is also posthumously awarded the first Golden Hat Award from the Academy of Country Music for his influence on country music

1985

5 Jan A TV special, *Elvis: One Night With You*—a complete record of one of the performances taped for the NBC TV *Elvis* comeback special—is shown on Home Box Office cable TV and repeated throughout the month

Aug A syndicated TV special, *Elvis: The Echo Will Never Die*, features people who knew or worked with Elvis

1986

Feb Elvis is, posthumously, one of the first to be inducted into the Rock and Roll Hall of Fame in Cleveland, Ohio

1987

Aug On a phone-in run by *USA Today*, fans vote "Suspicious Minds" their No. 1 favorite Elvis song, with "Love Me Tender" No. 2

Elvis is posthumously granted an Award of Merit at the American Music Awards

1988

The 1956 recording of "Hound Dog" is inducted into the NARAS Hall of Fame

7–8 Feb A mini-series, *Elvis and Me*, based on Priscilla's book about her life with Elvis, is broadcast on ABC TV and becomes the highest-rated TV movie of 1987/88

Oct Lisa Marie marries musician Danny Keough

1989

NBC TV broadcasts *Elvis: Comeback 68*—a repeat of the program broadcast on December 3, 1968, which *TV Guide* describes as the best rock performance ever on television

29 May Lisa Marie and her husband have a daughter, Danielle Riley

1990

May The first Elvis Awards ceremony is held in New York, and Eric Clapton is named Best Rock Guitarist

1992

A two-volume video collection is re-edited and broadcast as *Elvis, The Great Performances (Televised Version)*, with Priscilla hosting it from Graceland

A video, *Elvis, The Lost Performances*, is released, with unseen footage from the films of his concerts

22 Jan A two-hour TV special, *The Elvis Conspiracy—The Elvis Files*, is broadcast; it alleges that Elvis went undercover for the FBI and is still alive

6 Apr A postcard ballot is held to choose which image of Elvis is to be used on a US postage stamp; an image of a young Elvis is chosen. *US News & World Report* says that revenue from sales of the Elvis stamp is expected to reach $20 million. The stamp is released in January 1993 and becomes the best-selling stamp in US postal history

21 Oct Lisa Marie and her husband have a second child, a boy named Benjamin Storm

1993

A video documentary, *Elvis in Hollywood*, is released, with footage from the first four films, out-takes and interviews with those involved at the time

A TV special, *America Comes to Graceland*, about Elvis's life and legacy, is broadcast in the US

1 Feb Lisa Marie turns 25 and is entitled to take charge of her inheritance, but decides to found the Elvis Presley Trust to run the estate, with Priscilla and the National Bank of Commerce as co-trustees

1 Mar *People* magazine estimates that Elvis's estate is now worth nearly $100 million

1994

Lisa Marie divorces Danny Keough

26 May Michael Jackson and Lisa Marie are married in the Dominican Republic

1995

The 1956 recording of "Heartbreak Hotel" is inducted into the NARAS Hall of Fame

1996

Lisa Marie divorces Michael Jackson

A virtual tour of Graceland is released on CD

1997

At the Mid-South Coliseum in Memphis, *Elvis in Concert 97* features Elvis on video accompanied live on stage by over 30 of his former band members and the Memphis Symphony Orchestra; a digitally remastered video is also shown, with Lisa Marie singing "Don't Cry, Daddy' with Elvis

An official video tour, *Elvis Presley's Graceland*, is released

1998

The 1954 recording of "That's All Right, Mama" is inducted into the NARAS Hall of Fame

Lisa Marie becomes owner and Chairman of the Board of Elvis Presley Enterprises, Inc., while Priscilla becomes Chairman of the Advisory Board

Elvis is posthumously inducted into the Country Music Hall of Fame

1999

The 1969 recording of "Suspicious Minds" is inducted into the NARAS Hall of Fame

Nov–Jan A two-part documentary, *He Touched Me: The Gospel Music of Elvis Presley*, is aired on TNN and the whole program is also released as two videos

2001

21 Sept *America The Beautiful*, a special CD single featuring Elvis singing three songs, enters the *Billboard* Hot 100 singles sales chart at No. 8; it peaks at No. 6 for two weeks in November

Dec Graceland is voted fourth Most Visited Historic House Museum in the United States, on the list compiled by the Almanac of Architecture and Design; Elvis is posthumously inducted into the Gospel Music Hall of Fame

2002

9 Jan It is announced that the Vaughan-Bassett Furniture Company has gone into partnership with Elvis Presley Enterprises, Inc. to manufacture an exclusive range of wood furniture to be known as the Elvis Presley Collection; the collection is launched later that year

A remix of Presley's "A Little Less Conversation" (credited as Elvis Vs JXL) was used in a Nike advertising campaign during the World Cup

2005

Forbes magazine named Presley the top-earning deceased celebrity for the fifth year running, with a gross income of $45 million. In 2009, he was ranked fourth

Acknowledgments

All photographs in this book are reproduced by kind permission of Corbis, Getty Images, and the Aquarius Collection Limited. Thanks to all the photographers who have contributed and the film and television companies who have provided the libraries with promotional stills.

Page 1 Bettman Corbis
Page 2 Bettman Corbis
Page 3 Bettman Corbis
Page 4 Bettman Corbis
Page 6 John Stringer Collection/Corbis

Chapter 1
8 Getty Images/Twentieth Century Fox
12 Bettman Corbis
13 Getty Images
14 (t) Getty Images
14 (b) Getty Images
15 Getty Images
16 Corbis
17 Bettman Corbis
18 (t) Getty Images
18 (b) Corbis
19 Getty Images
20 Getty Images
21 Corbis
22 Bettman Corbis
23 Bettman Corbis
24 Aquarius Collection
25 (t) Bettman Corbis
25 (b) Bettman Corbis
26–7 Bettman Corbis
28 (t) Bettman Corbis
28 (b) Bettman Corbis
30–1 Bettman Corbis
32 Bettman Corbis
33 Bettman Corbis
34 Twentieth-Century Fox/ Bettman Corbis
35 Twentieth-Century Fox/ Bettman Corbis

36 Twentieth-Century Fox/ Bettman Corbis
37 (t)Twentieth-Century Fox/ Bettman Corbis
37 (b) Twentieth-Century Fox/ Bettman Corbis
38–9 Twentieth-Century Fox Bettman Corbis
40 Twentieth-Century Fox/ Bettman Corbis
41 Bettman Corbis
42 Bettman Corbis
43 Bettman Corbis
44 Bettman Corbis
45 (t) Bettman Corbis
46 Bettman Corbis
47 (t) Bettman Corbis
47 (b) Bettman Corbis
48 Bettman Corbis
49 Bettman Corbis
50 Bettman Corbis
51 Getty Images

Chapter 2
52 Bettman Corbis
56 Paramount/Getty Images
57 Paramount/Getty Images
58 (t) Bettman Corbis
58 (b) Bettman Corbis
59 Paramount/Bettman Corbis
60 (t) Bettman Corbis
60 (b) MGM/Bettman Corbis
61 Bettman Corbis
62 MGM/Bettman Corbis
63 (t) Underwood & Underwood/Corbis
64 MGM/Bettman Corbis
65 MGM/Bettman Corbis
66/67 MGM/Bettman Corbis

68 MGM/Getty Images
69 MGM/Getty Images
70 (t) Bettman Corbis
70 (b) Seattle Post-Intelligence Collection.
        Museum of History and Industry/Corbis
71 Bettman Corbis
72 Bettman Corbis
73 Bettman Corbis
74 Bettman Corbis
75 (t) Bettman Corbis
75 (b) Seattle Post-Intelligence Collection.
        Museum of History and Industry/Corbis

Chapter 3
78 Bettman Corbis
80 (t) Bettman Corbis
80 (b) Bettman Corbis
81 Bettman Corbis
82 Bettman Corbis
83 Bettman Corbis
84 Bettman Corbis
85 Bettman Corbis
86 Bettman Corbis
87 Time&Life, Getty Images
88 Bettman Corbis
89 (t) Bettman Corbis
89 (b) Bohnacker/dpa/Corbis
90–1 Bettman Corbis
92 (t) Bettman Corbis
92 (b) Bettman Corbis
93 Bettman Corbis
94 Bettman Corbis
95 (t) Bettman Corbis

95 (b) Bettman Corbis
96 Bettman Corbis
97 Bettman Corbis
98(t) Bohnacker/dpa/Corbis
98 (b) Bettman Corbis
100 Ochs/Corbis
101 Bettman Corbis
102 (t) Corbis
102 (b) Corbis
103 Bettman Corbis
104 Bettman Corbis
105 Bettman Corbis
106 (t) Bettman Corbis
106 (b) Corbis
107 (t) Bettman Corbis
107 (b) Bettman Corbis
108 Bettman Corbis
109 (t) Bettman Corbis
109 (b) Bettman Corbis
110 Bettman Corbis
111 (t) Bettman Corbis
111 (b) Bettman Corbis
112 Bettman Corbis
113 Bettman Corbis
114 (t) Bettman Corbis
114 (b) Bettman Corbis
114 Bettman Corbis
115 Bettman Corbis
116 (t) Bettman Corbis
117 Bettman Corbis
118-9 Paramount/ Bettman Corbis
120 Paramount/ Bettman Corbis
121 (t) Twentieth-Century Fox/Aquarius
121 (b) Twentieth-Century Fox/ Aquarius
122 Twentieth-Century Fox/ Aquarius
123 Twentieth-Century Fox/ Aquarius
124 Bettman Corbis
125 (t) Bettman Corbis
125 (b) Bettman Corbis

Chapter 4
126 Twentieth-Century Fox/Aquarius
130 Twentieth-Century Fox/Aquarius
131 (t) Twentieth-Century Fox/Aquarius
131 (b) Paramount/Bettman Corbis
132 Bettman Corbis
133 (t) Paramount/Bettman Corbis
133 (b)Ochs/Getty Images
134 Paramount/Bettman Corbis
135 Paramount/Bettman Corbis
136 United Artists/Bettman Corbis
137 Bettman Corbis
138 United Artists/Aquarius
139 (t) Paramount/ Bettman Corbis
139 (b) Paramount/Aquarius
140 Seattle Post-Intelligence Collection.
      Museum of History and Industry/Corbis
141 Seattle Post-Intelligence Collection.
      Museum of History and Industry/Corbis
142-3 MGM/Getty Images
144 MGM/Bettman Corbis
145 (t) MGM/Bettman Corbis

145 (b) MGM/Bettman Corbis
146-7 MGM/Bettman Corbis
148 MGM/Bettman Corbis
149 Bettman Corbis
150 Allied Artists/Bettman Corbis
151 (t) Allied Artists/Bettman Corbis
151 (b) Allied Artists/Bettman Corbis
152 Paramount/Aquarius
153 (t) Allied Artists/Aquarius
153 (b) Allied Artists/Aquarius
154 Allied Artists/Aquarius
155 (t) Allied Artists/Aquarius
155 (b) Allied Artists/Aquarius
156 (t) Allied Artists/Aquarius
157 (b) Allied Artists/Aquarius
158 Bettman Corbis
159 Paramount/Bettman Corbis
160-161 MGM/Bettman Corbis
162 MGM/Corbis
163 (t) United Artists/Aquarius
163 (b) United Artists/Aquarius
164 MGM/Aquarius
165 United Artists/Aquarius
166 Sunset Boulevard/United Artists/Corbis
167 Bettman Corbis
168 Bettman Corbis
169 Bettman Corbis
170-171 Getty Images
172 (t) Bettman Corbis
172 (b) Bettman Corbis
173 Bettman Corbis
174 MGM/Aquarius
175 (t) MGM/Aquarius
175 (b) MGM/Aquarius
176 MGM/Aquarius
177 MGM/Aquarius
178 Bettman Corbis
179 (t) Bettman Corbis
179 (b) Bettman Corbis
180 MGM/Aquarius
181 Bettman Corbis
182 (t) MGM/Aquarius
182 (b) MGM/Aquarius
183 MGM/Aquarius
184 MGM/Aquarius
185 (t) National General/Aquarius
185 (b) Bettman Corbis
186-187 Getty Images
188 (t) MGM/Aquarius
188 (b) Aquarius
188 MGM/Aquarius
190 Bettman Corbis
191 Bettman Corbis
192 Ochs/Getty Images
193 Ochs/Getty Images
194 MCA/Universal/Redferns/Getty Images
195 (t) MCA/Universal/Redferns/Getty Images
195 (b) MCA/Universal/Redferns/Getty Images
196 (t) Getty Images
196 (b) Getty Images
197 Bettman Corbis

Chapter 5
198 Sam Emerson/Sygma
202 MGM/Bettman Corbis
203 (t) MGM/Bettman Corbis
203 (b) Korody/Sygma
204 MGM/Bettman Corbis
205 (t) Corbis
205 (b) Sam Emerson/Sgyma
206 Jeff Albertson/Corbis
207 Sam Emerson/Sygma
208 Bettman Corbis
209 (t) Jeff Albertson/Corbis
209 (b) Jeff Albertson/Corbis
210 Corbis
211 (t) Corbis
211 (b) Jeff Albertson/Corbis
212 (r) Bettman Corbis
212 (l) Bettman Corbis
213 Bettman Corbis
214 Bettman Corbis
215 Bettman Corbis
216 Getty Images
217 Getty Images
218 Bettman Corbis
219 (t) Frank Carroll Sygma
219 (b) Bettman Corbis

Chapter 6
220 Bettman Corbis
223 Bettman Corbis
224 (t) Bettman Corbis
224 (b) Bettman Corbis
225 (t) Bettman Corbis
225 (b) Bettman Corbis
226 (t) Bettman Corbis
226 (bl) Alain Nogues/Sygma
226 (br) Kevin Fleming/Corbis
227 Henry Diltz/Corbis
228–9 Arthur Grace/Corbis
229 inset Henry Diltz (Corbis)
230 (t) Philip Gould/Corbis
230 (b) Raymond Gehman/Corbis
231 Kevin Fleming/Corbis

Chronology
232 Getty Images
237 Twentieth-Century Fox/Aquarius
243 Bettman Corbis
246 Bettman Corbis
250 Bettman Corbis
253 Twentieth-Century Fox/Aquarius
256 Getty Images/Twentieth-Century Fox

Every effort has been made to ensure that the copyright details shown are correct, but if there are any inaccuracies, please contact the publisher.